The Magic of Soy

Healthy Cooking with Soy Protein

Presented by

GeniSoy Products

Book Publishing Company

Summertown, Tennessee

Cover photos: Digital Imagery®
    Copyright 1999 PhotoDisk, Inc.

Cover design: Reka Design

Interior design: Warren Jefferson, Cynthia Holzapfel

02 01 00   5 4 3 2 1

Published in the United States by   Book Publishing Company
                                     PO Box 99
                                     Summertown, TN 38483
                                     888-260-8458
                                     www.bookpubco.com

ISBN 1-57067-090-0

Magic of soy : healthy cooking with soy protein / presented by GeniSoy Products
            p. cm.
        Includes bibliographical references and index.
        ISBN 1-57067-090-0 (alk. paper)
        1. Soy proteins--Therapeutic use. 2. Cookery (Soybeans) I. GeniSoy Products
        RM666.S59 S66 2000
        641.5'63--dc21   00-020295

Calculations for the nutritional analyses in this book are based on the average number of servings listed with the recipes and the average amount of an ingredient, if a range is called for. Calculations are rounded up to the nearest gram. If two options for an ingredient are listed, the first one is used. Not included are optional ingredients, serving suggestions, or fat used for frying, unless the amount of fat is specified in the recipe.

Contents

Experience the Magic of Soy

Welcome to the exciting and healthful world of soy! Whether you are new to soyfoods or have been eating them for years, you will be happy to know that there is good news about soy and your health. The Food & Drug Administration (FDA) has concluded that soy protein consumption (25 g per day) included in a diet low in saturated fat and cholesterol may reduce the risk of coronary artery disease by lowering blood cholesterol levels. In fact, the FDA has officially approved the use of the following health claim label on products that contain at least 6.25 grams of soy protein per serving and 3 grams or less of total fat (the fat requirement is waived for soyfoods that are 100 percent soy):

"Twenty-five grams of soy protein a day, as part of a diet low in saturated fat and cholesterol, may reduce the risk of heart disease."[1]

The GeniSoy products that meet these requirements proudly display this label along with the heart-healthy logo. Soy protein may also help in the prevention of cancer and osteoporosis and the relief of menopausal discomfort. These health benefits are strongly linked to phytonutrients in soy protein called isoflavones.

✳   ✳   ✳

About GeniSoy

GeniSoy Products Company was founded in 1997 after its parent company (MLO Products) began manufacturing isolated soy protein products for institutional research studies investigating soy's health benefits. Soon after these benefits were substantiated, the first GeniSoy products were developed to bring the health benefits of soy to the world in a form that was convenient, economical, and delicious. Since then, we've been committed to providing the highest quality, best tasting, and most affordable soy products available.

GeniSoy offers consumers a variety of soy protein products that includes GeniSoy Soy Protein Bars (including one non-fat and several low-fat baked bars), GeniSoy Chocolate and Vanilla Shakes, GeniSoy Natural Protein Powder, and assorted flavors of GeniSoy Soy Nuts, a crunchy, nut-like snack toasted without oil and containing 60% less fat than peanuts. The protein powder can be used in many recipes from smoothies to freshly baked muffins. Numerous recipes are found in the following section of this book.

GeniSoy uses only water-processed isolated soy protein from IPP Certified, non-GMO (nongenetically modified organism) soybeans. Water-processing preserves the naturally occurring levels of isoflavones found in soy (genistein and daidzein). Research has demonstrated isoflavones' antioxidant properties and numerous studies have demonstrated soy's ability to reduce the risk of heart disease by lowering blood cholesterol. Other studies suggest that soy products have the potential to reduce the risks of cancer and osteoporosis. The majority of these studies used the same isolated soy protein found in GeniSoy products.

Based in Fairfield, California, GeniSoy Products Company is dedicated to making nutritious and tasty soy-based products. It is part of a 35-year old company (MLO Products) that started making sports nutrition bars and protein powders in 1964. GeniSoy products can be found in your local natural food store or the natural foods section of your favorite supermarket.

About Soy

Soybeans have provided a major source of protein and other nutritional benefits to a large part of the world's population for literally thousands of years. With a protein content of approximately 38-40 percent protein, soybeans are one of the few plants that have protein equal in quality to animal protein sources, such as meat, dairy, and eggs. Soyfoods contain no cholesterol and some of them, such as many GeniSoy products, are fat-free. Soybeans are processed to make traditional soyfoods like soymilk and tofu, as well as ingredients that can be used in and added to a wide variety of foods and products. Soybean oil, for example, is the most widely consumed vegetable oil in the United States and is a major source of the vitamin E and lecithin sold as supplements. Another product called isolated soy protein is the main soy ingredient in GeniSoy products.

To make isolated soy protein, soybeans are processed by first removing their hulls. They are then flaked and defatted to make "white flakes," which can be either milled, alcohol-extracted, or processed with water. Milling creates defatted flour or grits. Alcohol extraction removes flavor compounds and sugars (that can cause intestinal gas) to make protein concentrates, which are 70 percent protein. Water processing removes sugars and flavor compounds and is then followed by precipitation and drying to make protein isolates, which are at least 90 percent protein.

The type of processing is important. Alcohol extraction, which is used to make most soy protein concentrates, removes alcohol-soluble substances, such as isoflavones and saponins that occur naturally in soy.

However, the water extraction method used to process most soy protein isolates leaves isoflavones and other alcohol-soluble substances intact.

The phytonutrients found in soy protein—like the isoflavones genistein and daidzein—are considered by most to be responsible for the observed health benefits, and these phytochemicals (plant chemicals) are found almost exclusively in soy. This has led some to extract the isoflavones and use them in supplement form. But many believe that the health benefits are maximized when the isoflavanones are consumed as part of soy protein. Other possible beneficial phytochemicals include saponins, phytic acid, and protease inhibitors.

There has been an increasing focus on soy's possible health benefits. A look at worldwide health statistics shows that Asian peoples typically enjoy much lower rates of many of the chronic diseases that plague the United States and other Western nations, such as heart disease, cancer, and osteoporosis. One striking difference between Eastern and Western diets is that soyfoods are a primary protein source in many Asian countries. The fact that Asian people lose their health advantage when they adopt Western eating habits has led researchers to look at the Asian diet for answers.

Soy and Heart Disease

When all the diseases of the heart and arteries are lumped together (i.e., heart attack, stroke, high blood pressure, etc.), they are called cardiovascular disease. Although progress has been made in the prevention and treatment of cardiovascular disease, it remains the number one killer of men and women in the United States, accounting for more than 40 percent of all deaths. Of all the cardiovascular diseases, heart disease, primarily heart attack, has received the most attention.

Many years of research have identified some of the most important factors in the development of heart disease. Atherosclerosis is one of the most frequent factors and is present in most heart attacks. It's a process where material called plaque builds up on an artery wall at a site where there is oxidative damage to arterial cells. Blood flow is reduced and complete blockage of plaque-narrowed arteries results in a heart attack.

Years ago, when researchers discovered that plaque consisted primarily of a lipid substance called cholesterol, they began to focus on finding ways to decrease the amount of cholesterol in the blood. Cholesterol travels in the blood in combination particles made up of fat and protein, the best known being low-density lipoprotein (LDL) and high-density lipoprotein (HDL). High blood levels of LDL contribute to plaque buildup by becoming oxidized by free radicals (unstable molecules that are missing an electron, making them highly reactive) and sticking to the arterial walls, making it a major risk factor for heart disease. However, high levels of HDL reduce the risk of heart disease by inhibiting the growth of plaque.

For years the emphasis in both prevention and treatment of heart disease has been to decrease the amount of LDL in the blood. Individuals with high LDL cholesterol are typically recommended to make several lifestyle changes, including changing their diet by reducing fat intake along with saturated fat and cholesterol.

Researchers have recently been investigating the possibility that some foods may protect against heart disease. One area of increasing interest is the potential role of soy-foods and soy protein in preventing and treating heart disease.

Prevention with Soy

In the summer of 1995, public interest in the health benefits of soy increased when noted researcher Dr. James Anderson and his associates published a ground-breaking compilation of research done on the effects of soy protein on human blood lipid levels. This compilation allowed researchers to combine the results of 38 smaller studies to strengthen and validate their findings. It was shown that consuming soy protein rather than animal protein significantly decreased blood levels of total cholesterol and LDL. (See Table 1 below.) Results also showed that soy protein was most effective in people at the highest risk level. The higher the initial levels of total and LDL cholesterol, the greater the amount of lowering.[2]

It is now widely accepted that soy protein consumption decreases high blood LDL levels. As little as

Table 1

Percent Change in Human Blood Levels of Cholesterol and Triglycerides

(comparing soy consumption to control diets)

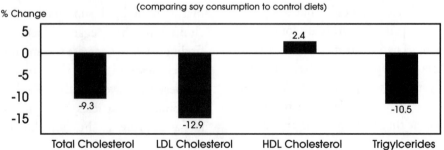

25 grams of soy protein per day has been shown to lower cholesterol in individuals with high cholesterol levels. A number of components in soy protein have been given credit for soy's ability to lower LDL. Experts don't know exactly what components of soy and soy protein provide these health benefits, but the components that have been most thoroughly investigated include:

- Isoflavones
- Amino acids
- Globulins
- Saponins
- Soy fiber
- Phytic acid
- Trypsin inhibitors

Isoflavones are a type of phytochemical (plant chemical). Some are classified as phytoestrogens because their chemical structure is similar to human estrogen. They act as weak estrogens in the body—apparently acting like the hormone in some circumstances and blocking its action in others. Estrogens are known to protect against heart disease in several ways, including decreasing LDL and increasing HDL. This may help explain the lower rate of heart disease in women before menopause. Genistein is the isoflavone most prevalent in soy. It's thought that it may play a role in the prevention of arterial wall changes that occur when atherosclerosis begins. Genistein may also interfere with the formation of blood clots that can lead to arterial blockage. In addition, genistein and daidzein, another soy isoflavone, are antioxidants, and researchers are investigating the possible role of soy isoflavones in reducing the oxidation of LDL, thus lowering its potential for causing heart disease.

The amount of isoflavones in soyfoods depends on a number of factors. Their levels in soybeans is affected largely by the type of soybean and the soil in which it is grown. Processing can also change isoflavone levels. The alcohol-extraction method most commonly used to make soy concentrates, for example, removes naturally occurring isoflavones. Water extraction, which is used to process most isolated soy protein, leaves the isoflavones intact.

Amino acids are the building blocks of proteins. Animal studies have shown that specific amino acids have different effects on blood cholesterol levels. The amino acid lysine, for example, raises cholesterol levels, while the amino acid arginine lowers them. The protein in soy has more arginine and less lysine than casein, the milk protein often used as an animal protein source in most studies. Researchers believe that the amino acid ratio in soy protein accounts for at least some of the cholesterol-lowering action.

Globulins are a specific type of protein. Human and animal studies suggest that certain globulins found in soy protein may decrease LDL levels.

Saponins have a chemical sensitivity to cholesterol and may act to lower blood cholesterol by either blocking its absorption in the small intestine or enhancing its excretion.[3]

Soy fiber can lower blood cholesterol, and it shares this lipid-lowering effect with many different types of fiber, such as bran, oats, and other grains that are not overly refined.

Other soy protein constituents under investigation for possible cholesterol-lowering effects are phytic acid and trypsin inhibitors.

Soy and Cancer

Evidence of soy isoflavones' protective effects from cancer comes from several sources. Some of the strongest and most convincing evidence comes from well-designed population studies that demonstrate the role of soy isoflavones in cancer prevention. Review of many studies confirms that vegetarians and Asians have a low incidence of breast and prostate cancer. Also, the lower incidence of breast cancer in Singapore and Hong Kong has been directly linked to dietary intake of soy, with isoflavones being the principal agents responsible for the reduced risk. Many other studies of Asian populations also link a lower risk for other types of cancer to their consumption of soyfoods. Experiments in animals with transplanted tumors, especially tumors dependent on hormonal activity for growth, show that cancer growth is suppressed. And Dr. Stephen Barnes and his colleagues from the University of Alabama showed that modest amounts of soybeans added to the diet of rats caused a 50 percent reduction in breast cancer.[4]

Soy and Osteoporosis

Osteoporosis is a very serious disease in which bones become brittle and can break easily. It has been recognized as an important public health problem and has become a major cause of disability in the elderly, with older women being the fastest growing segment. Osteoporosis currently affects the lives of more than 25 million people in the United States.[5] It is the principal underlying cause of the estimated 1.5 million bone fractures of the hip, spine, wrist, and other sites which occur each year[6] at an annual cost of $10 to 20 billion.[7] It is estimated that more than half of all women and about one third of men will have fractures caused by osteoporosis during their lives.[8]

Bone is connective tissue that becomes hard when minerals

(primarily calcium) are deposited on it. Although bone doesn't look very active, it is constantly being built up and broken down. Bones become weak when the amount being broken down exceeds the amount being rebuilt. Some factors that influence bone strength are calcium intake, exercise, and the presence of the hormone estrogen, which protects bone from losing too much calcium.

The most common form of osteoporosis occurs in women after menopause. Bone quickly begins to lose calcium and breaks down in response to the drastic reduction in estrogen. Estrogen replacement therapy can reduce the risk of osteoporosis; however, it may not be appropriate for some women, and many choose not to take hormones. Women give various reasons for not wanting estrogen replacement therapy, including trust that "nature knows best" and that you should just "tough it out." They also have doubts about the effectiveness of estrogen supplements, anxiety about their immediate side effects (such as water retention and reappearance of menstrual bleeding), and concern about their possible long-term effects, primarily a fear of cancer.[9] One large study of postmenopausal women showed that only about 17 percent were taking estrogen, 27 percent had taken estrogen in the past and stopped, and 55 percent had never taken estrogen therapy.[10] Observations that Asian women have lower rates of osteoporosis while using much less hormone replacement therapy[11] and consuming less calcium,[12] have led researchers to take a closer look at the role of soyfoods in the Asian diet.

Prevention with Soy

One issue in bone health appears to be the type and amount of protein consumed. Research shows that as protein intake increases, the amount of calcium excreted in urine increases.[13] However, not all proteins have the same effect on calcium. Compared with animal protein, vegetable protein (such as soy) causes a much smaller amount of calcium excretion, leaving more available to strengthen bone.[14]

Americans eat a lot of protein, which may be one reason we have a higher recommended calcium intake than people in other countries. Not only do we traditionally eat a lot of protein, but much of it comes from animal sources. The ongoing Nurses Health Study has shown a greater number of forearm fractures as animal protein intake increases.[15] No such association has been found with vegetable protein intake.

A second issue is that studies of soy isoflavones, especially genistein, show that they act like a weak form of estrogen. As such, isoflavones may be able to preserve and improve bone health. A recent study of postmenopausal women compared the effects of consuming either soy protein or dairy protein on bone weight and on the amount of mineral present to strengthen bone.[16] The results showed that women who consumed soy protein with naturally occurring isoflavones had significant increases in bone weight and in the amount of mineral in their bones, especially their spines, compared to women consuming dairy protein. Research also indicates that isoflavones may decrease the breakdown of bone.

There is also much interest in ipriflavone, a synthetic isoflavone similar in structure to the soy isoflavones. This compound is used to treat osteoporosis in Japan, and is currently being evaluated in European and American studies.[17] One of the active compounds formed when ipriflavone is metabolized in the body is daidzein, an isoflavone found in soy.[18]

Soy and Menopause

Although menopause is much less serious than heart disease, cancer, and osteoporosis, women experiencing it can be very miserable. In many women, menopause discomforts can continue for many years. These include hot flashes, insomnia, heavy sweating (especially at night, which further contributes to insomnia), headaches, mood swings, nervousness and irritability, depression, and vaginal dryness and soreness, which make intercourse painful. Although women can reduce postmenopausal discomforts by taking estrogen, the vast majority choose not to have this hormone replacement therapy.

There are noticeable differences in menopausal discomforts between women from the East and the West. For example, it is estimated that while up to 85 percent of women in Western cultures have hot flashes and night sweats, less than 10 percent of Japanese women have hot flashes and less than 4 percent have night sweats. One Japanese-born woman commented that she had never heard of hot flashes until she came to the United States and wasn't aware of a Japanese word for this condition. Although there may be several explanations for these differences between women in the East and West, researchers have focused on the possible effects of phytoestrogens found in the soyfoods so abundant in the Japanese diet.

Prevention with Soy

Of the limited number of studies done to examine the possible effect of soy phytoestrogens on menopausal discomforts, a research study in England showed that post-menopausal women consuming a soy protein drink had fewer hot flashes and lower cholesterol levels than a placebo group. Also, preliminary results from several studies in Australia indicate that women consuming soy had a 50 percent reduction in the number of hot flashes. One short-term study of 51 menopausal women showed a slight decrease in discomforts, accompanied by improvements in blood cholesterol and blood pressure. These benefits were achieved apparently without the negative side effects of estrogen replacement therapy such as increased blood triglycerides and tissue changes in the breast and endometrium.

It seems reasonable for women suffering from menopausal discomforts to take advantage of the possible benefits of adding soy-foods that contain phytoestrogens into their daily diets. The research is on their side, and soyfoods have a long track record of safety, having been consumed in Eastern countries without negative effects for thousands of years. Because research on the health benefits of soyfoods and their naturally occurring phyto-estrogens is increasing, there should be a steady stream of information about the connection between soy phytoestrogens and menopausal discomforts in the future.

Choosing Soy Products

Whenever exciting research like that on soy and soy isoflavones comes along, there is a tendency to look for a quick fix. Why bother eating soyfoods? Why not just get isoflavones in a pill?

There are several reasons why consuming actual foods based on soy or soy protein is better. We know that consuming soyfoods protects against some diseases, but we don't know for certain what in soy actually provides that protection. Is it a single isoflavone? Is it several of them working together? To be effective, do the isoflavones need to be in the same proportion as they appear in soyfoods? Could the benefit be due to something else in soy protein that has yet to be identified? Don't forget what happened in beta-carotene research. Many studies had shown lower rates of lung cancer in individuals consuming fruits and vegetables rich in beta carotene, a precursor to vitamin A. The scientific world was shocked when a study using a supplement of beta-carotene failed to show any benefit.

Remember, not all soyfoods are equal! Some foods are made from alcohol-extracted soy concentrates that have had their isoflavones and other alcohol-soluble phytochemicals removed during processing. The research that has demonstrated the healthful benefits of soy has used foods made with soy containing naturally occurring isoflavones, not pills containing phytochemicals. Phytochemicals that are healthful in the amounts naturally found in soyfoods may not be as safe in the abnormally large amounts that might be consumed in pill form.

Make Room for Soy

Add soyfoods with their naturally occurring components to your daily diet. And don't worry if you're not a big fan of unfamiliar foods such as tofu and soymilk. Instead, take advantage of the growing number of natural soy-based products that are similar to the foods you know and love.

GeniSoy uses isolated soy protein in its soy protein powder, soy protein shakes, and soy protein bars. Soy protein is one of the highest quality soyfoods and it contains no cholesterol or fat. And don't forget our Soynuts, which are toasted soybeans that are naturally lower in fat than similar snacks like peanuts.

All GeniSoy products have the IPP, NON-GMO label to show that the soy protein we select for our products comes from certified non-GMO soybeans. IPP stands for Identity Preservation Program, and it involves starting out with a soybean that is certified to be non-GMO. Then, in order to safeguard against the accidental addition of GMO to these non-GMO soybeans, the special crop must be controlled at every stage—planting, harvesting, transportation, storage, processing, and production of soy-based ingredients and the foods that contain them.

With research studies showing the health benefits of soyfoods with their naturally occurring isoflavones, isn't it time you add some soyfoods to your diet?

Notes

1. Federal Register of the United States, Department of Health and Human Services, Food and Drug Administration. 21 CFR Part 101 - Food Labeling: Health Claims; *Soy Protein and Coronary Heart Disease; Final Rule*. Docket No. 98P-0683, CFSAN 9990, October 26, 1999, Volume 64, p. 57699-57733.

2. Anderson, J. W., B. M. Johnstone, and M. E Cook-Newell, "Meta-analysis of the effects of soy protein intake on serum lipids," *New England Journal of Medicine* 333 (1995): 276-282.

3. See note above, p. 69.

4. Holt, Stephen, M.D. *The Soy Revolution: The Food of the Next Millenium*. (New York: M. Evans and Company, Inc., 1998), p. 46-47.

5. NIH Consensus Development Panel on Optimal Calcium Intake, "Optimum Calcium Intake," *Journal of the American Medical Association* 272, no. 24 (1994): p. 1942-1948.

6. See note 4 above.

7. Lindsay, R. "The Burden of Osteoporosis: Cost," American Journal of Medicine. 1995, Volume 98, Suppl. 2A, p. 9 S11S

8. Ross, P. D., "Osteoporosis. Frequency, consequences and risk factors," *Archives of Internal Medicine* 156 (1996): 1399-1411.

9. Wardell, D. W., and J. C. Engebretson, "Women's anticipations of hormonal replacement therapy," *Maturitas* 22 (1995): 177-183.

10. Salamone L. M., and others, "Estrogen Replacement Therapy, A Survey of Older Women's Attitudes," *Archives of Internal Medicine* 156, no.12 (1996): 1293-1297.

11. Fujita, T., "Clinical Guidelines for the Treatment of Osteoporosis in Japan," abstract in *Calcified Tissue International* 59, Suppl 1 (1996): 3437.

12. Messina, Mark, and Virginia Messina. *The Simple Soybean and Your Health*. (Garden City Park, New York: Avery Publishing Group, 1994).

13. Kerstetter, J. E., and L. H. Allen, "Dietary Protein Increases Urinary Calcium," *Journal of Nutrition* 120 (1989): 134-136.

14. Breslau, N. A., and others, "Relationship of Animal Protein-Rich Diet to Kidney Stone Formation and Calcium Metabolism," *Journal of Clinical Endocrinology and Metabolism* 140 (1988): 140-146.

15. Feskanich, D., and others, "Protein Consumption and Bone Fractures in Women," *American Journal of Epidemiology* 143, no. 5 (1996): 472-479.

16. Erdman, J. W., and others, "Short-Term Effects of Soybean Isoflavones on Bone in Post-menopausal Women," abstract for the Second International Symposium on the role of Soy in Preventing and Treating Chronic Disease, Brussels, Belgium, September 15-18, 1996.

17. Reginster, J. Y., "Miscellaneous and experimental agents," *American Journal of the Medical Sciences* 313 (1997): 3340.

Also see note 10 above.

18. Brandi, M. L., "Flavonoids: Biochemical Effects and Therapeutic Applications," *Bone and Mineral* 19, Suppl. (1992): S3-S14.

Smoothies
and Shakes

THE
MAGIC
OF SOY

Orange Kiwi Smoothie

Yield: 1 serving

Combine all the ingredients in a blender, and process until smooth.

1 ripe banana

1 kiwi

¾ cup orange juice

1 scoop GeniSoy Natural Protein Powder (¼ cup)

Crushed ice

Per serving: Calories 335, Total Protein 30 g, Soy Protein 25 g, Carbohydrates 54 g, Fat 0 g, Sodium 297 mg

Raspberry Splash

Yield: 1 serving

Combine all the ingredients in a blender, and process until smooth.

1 cup orange juice

¼ cup raspberries

1 scoop GeniSoy Natural Protein Powder (¼ cup)

Crushed ice

Per serving: Calories 227, Total Protein 29 g, Soy Protein 25 g, Carbohydrates 30 g, Fat 0 g, Sodium 293 mg

Moss's Smoothie

Yield: 1 serving

1 cup Dole Pineapple/Orange/Strawberry Juice

1 scoop GeniSoy Natural Protein Powder or GeniSoy Natural Vanilla Shake Powder (¼ cup)

3 or 4 frozen strawberries

¼ to ⅓ cup tofu

Combine all the ingredients in a blender, and process until smooth, approximately 1 minute.

Per serving: Calories 294, Total Protein 32 g, Soy Protein 30 g, Carbohydrates 35 g, Fat 3 g, Sodium 306 mg

Rice Delight

Yield: 1 serving

1 cup rice milk

¼ cup raspberries

1 scoop GeniSoy Natural Protein Powder (¼ cup)

Crushed ice

Combine all the ingredients in a blender, and process until smooth.

Per serving: Calories 245, Total Protein 28 g, Soy Protein 25 g, Carbohydrates 31 g, Fat 2 g, Sodium 380 mg

Tropical Paradise

Yield: 1 serving

Combine all the ingredients in a blender, and process until smooth.

½ cup pineapple juice

½ cup orange juice

½ kiwi

1 scoop GeniSoy Natural Vanilla Shake Powder (¼ cup)

Crushed ice

Per serving: Calories 337, Total Protein 16 g, Soy Protein 14 g, Carbohydrates 66 g, Fat 0 g, Sodium 188 mg

Coco Cooler

Yield: 1 serving

Combine all the ingredients in a blender, and process until smooth.

1 cup soymilk

½ teaspoon carob powder

1 scoop GeniSoy Natural Chocolate Shake Powder (¼ cup)

Crushed ice

Per serving: Calories 204, Total Protein 20 g, Soy Protein 20 g, Carbohydrates 23 g, Fat 5 g, Sodium 200 mg

Southern Spritzer

Yield: 1 serving

½ cup sparkling mineral water

¼ cup pear juice

1½ teaspoons blackstrap
  molasses

1 scoop GeniSoy Natural Vanilla
  Shake Powder (¼ cup)

Crushed ice

Combine all the ingredients in a blender, and process until smooth.

Per serving: Calories 180, Total Protein 14 g, Soy Protein 14 g, Carbohydrates 30 g, Fat 0 g, Sodium 192 mg

Country Raspberry

Yield: 1 serving

1 cup apple cider

¼ cup raspberries

1 scoop GeniSoy Natural Protein
  Powder (¼ cup)

Crushed ice (optional)

Combine all the ingredients in a blender, and process until smooth. This drink can also be served hot.

Per serving: Calories 231, Total Protein 27 g, Soy Protein 25 g, Carbohydrates 32 g, Fat 0 g, Sodium 297 mg

Fruit Smoothie

Yield: 1 serving

Combine all the ingredients in a blender, and process until smooth.

1 cup chopped fresh peaches

1 cup soy yogurt

1 frozen banana

½ cup frozen blueberries

1 scoop GeniSoy Natural Protein Powder (¼ cup)

½ teaspoon vanilla

Sweetener, to taste

Per serving: Calories 381, Total Protein 35 g, Soy Protein 31 g, Carbohydrates 51 g, Fat 5 g, Sodium 326 mg

Vegan Eggnog

Yield: 10 *servings*

This "eggnog" will please even those who say they don't like soymilk. It's not too thick and cloying—a very refreshing drink any time of year. Make the "eggnog" ahead of time, then blend with the ice cubes right before serving.

2 (12.3-ounce) packages extra-firm silken tofu, crumbled

2 cups soymilk

⅔ cup sugar

2 scoops GeniSoy Natural Vanilla Shake Powder (½ cup)

¼ teaspoon salt

1 cup cold water

1 cup rum or brandy (or apple juice with rum or brandy flavoring, to taste)

4½ teaspoons pure vanilla extract

20 ice cubes

Freshly grated nutmeg

Place the crumbled tofu and soymilk in a blender with the sugar, protein powder, and salt. Process until very smooth. Scrape this into a large bowl or pitcher, and whisk in the water, rum or brandy, and vanilla. Mix well, cover, and refrigerate until serving time.

To serve, blend half of the mixture in the blender with 10 of the ice cubes until frothy. Repeat with the other half. Serve in glasses with nutmeg sprinkled on top.

Per serving: Calories 166, Total Protein 6 g, Soy Protein 6 g, Carbohydrates 18 g, Fat 1 g, Sodium 107 mg

Strawberry-Almond Soy Smoothie

Yield: 2 servings

Process all the ingredients in a blender until very smooth.

10 medium or 5 large frozen strawberries, chopped

1 cup soymilk

½ cup regular or silken tofu

1 scoop GeniSoy Natural Protein Powder (¼ cup)

2 tablespoons unbleached sugar or grade A light maple syrup

¼ to ½ teaspoon pure almond extract

Per serving: Calories 209, Total Protein 20 g, Soy Protein 20 g, Carbohydrates 19 g, Fat 5 g, Sodium 166 mg

Triple Soy Chocolate Milkshake

Yield: 2 servings

 o ahead and indulge! Creamy and frosty, but low in fat and rich in soy. For the richest flavor, use Dutch cocoa. Note: If your blender can't process ice cubes, place them in a plastic or burlap bag and crush them with a hammer first.

1 cup soymilk

½ cup medium-firm tofu or firm silken tofu

1 scoop GeniSoy Natural Chocolate Shake Powder (¼ cup)

¼ cup unbleached sugar, or to taste

2 tablespoons unsweetened Dutch cocoa powder

1 teaspoon vanilla, or ½ teaspoon peppermint extract

10 ice cubes

Combine all the ingredients, except the ice cubes, in a blender, and process until smooth. Add the ice cubes 2 at a time, blending briefly after each addition. When all are added, blend until the mixture is smooth and thick. Pour into glasses and serve immediately.

Per serving: Calories 259, Total Protein 16 g, Soy Protein 14 g, Carbohydrates 37 g, Fat 5 g, Sodium 106 mg

Easy Nondairy Hot Cocoa

Yield: 1 serving

Of course, you can just heat up your favorite chocolate-flavored soymilk, but if you have only plain soymilk in the house you can flavor it in different ways. For a dark, rich-tasting brew, use Dutch cocoa; for a milder drink, use regular cocoa powder. Soy protein isolate powder makes this very creamy.

Combine all the ingredients in a blender. Remove the plastic center part of the blender lid, and cover it with a folded tea towel before blending. This prevents steam build-up inside the blender which can cause hot liquid to explode. Blend until smooth. Pour into a mug and serve immediately.

Microwave Option

Use cold soymilk. Pour all the ingredients into a large microwave-safe mug (large enough to prevent boil-overs), and microwave on high for 1½ to 2 minutes. Whisk before serving.

1 cup very hot soymilk

½ tablespoon unsweetened cocoa powder

1 tablespoon unbleached sugar

1 tablespoon GeniSoy Natural Chocolate Shake Powder

¼ teaspoon vanilla, or ⅛ teaspoon almond or peppermint extract

Per serving: Calories 165, Total Protein 10 g, Soy Protein 9 g, Carbohydrates 21 g, Fat 5 g, Sodium 73 mg

Lassi

Yield: 6 to 8 servings

This Indian yogurt and fruit drink can be made with tofu and lemon juice so successfully that no one will know the difference. This makes a great snack or dessert anytime, and many combinations are possible

1⅓ cups chopped pineapple, or 1 cup frozen pineapple concentrate

2⅔ cups cold water plus ¼ cup sweetener, or 3 cups of your favorite fruit juice

1 cup crumbled firm silken tofu

1½ scoops GeniSoy Natural Protein Powder (6 tablespoons)

¼ cup lemon juice

12 ice cubes

Place all the ingredients, except the ice cubes, in a blender, and process until smooth.

Add as many of the ice cubes as your blender will hold, and grind up with the mixture until frothy.

Place any remaining ice cubes in serving glasses, and pour over the blended mixture. Serve immediately.

Per serving: Calories 104, Total Protein 8 g, Soy Protein 8 g, Carbohydrates 14 g, Fat 1 g, Sodium 77 mg

Banana-Chocolate Shake

Yield: 1 *serving*

Carob is an excellent substitute for chocolate. It is a naturally sweet bean that has a rich, deep, chocolate-like taste and contains small amounts of protein, phosphorus, and calcium.

Place all the ingredients in a blender, and process until the mixture is very smooth and creamy. Serve chilled or warm.

1 cup soymilk

1 medium-size ripe (fresh or frozen) banana, chunked

2 teaspoons unsweetened cocoa powder

1 scoop GeniSoy Natural Chocolate Shake Powder (¼ cup)

1 tablespoon pure maple syrup

¼ teaspoon vanilla extract

Per serving: Calories 369, Total Protein 22 g, Soy Protein 20 g, Carbohydrates 59 g, Fat 5 g, Sodium 204 mg

Creamsicle Frappé

Yield: 2 servings

A wonderful drink inspired by a favorite childhood dessert.

1 cup orange juice, or ¼ cup frozen orange juice concentrate plus ¾ cup ice water

½ cup firm silken tofu

½ cup ice water

1 scoop GeniSoy Natural Vanilla Shake Powder (¼ cup)

2 tablespoons frozen orange juice concentrate

¼ to ½ teaspoon vanilla extract

Place all the ingredients in a blender, and process until the mixture is very smooth and creamy. Serve at once.

Tip: For a special presentation, serve the frappé in tall, frosty glasses with straws, garnished with thin slices of fresh orange and/or fresh mint leaves.

Per serving: Calories 194, Total Protein 13 g, Soy Protein 12 g, Carbohydrates 31 g, Fat 2 g, Sodium 117 mg

Cappuccino Milkshakes

Yield: 1 serving

1 serving cooled espresso

½ cup cold plain, vanilla, carob, or chocolate soymilk

1 tablespoon GeniSoy Natural Protein Powder, GeniSoy Natural Chocolate Shake Powder, or GeniSoy Natural Vanilla Shake Powder

1 big scoop soy frozen dessert (in any flavor that goes well with coffee)

Pour the cooled espresso into a blender, and process with the rest of the ingredients. When smooth, pour into a tall glass and serve with a straw.

Breakfast

THE MAGIC OF SOY

French Toast

Yield: 6 pieces

Serve warm with applesauce, fruit-sweetened preserves, or pure maple syrup.

Place the protein powder, nutritional yeast flakes, salt, cinnamon, and nutmeg in a medium bowl, and stir with a dry whisk until well blended. Pour the soymilk into the flour mixture, and whisk vigorously until well blended. Let the batter sit for 10 minutes.

Oil a skillet or griddle, and place it over medium-high heat. Mix the batter again. Dip the bread slices, one at a time, into the batter, making sure that each piece is well saturated. Cook 3 to 5 minutes, or until the bottom is lightly brown, then turn over and cook the other side until golden brown.

Tip: This french toast tends to stick to the pan during cooking. Use a nonstick pan for the best results, or be sure to oil the pan well between batches.

2 tablespoons GeniSoy Natural Protein Powder or GeniSoy Natural Vanilla Shake Powder

1 teaspoon nutritional yeast flakes

¼ teaspoon salt

Pinch of cinnamon and nutmeg

1 cup plain or vanilla soymilk

6 slices whole grain bread

Per piece: Calories 72, Total Protein 5 g, Soy Protein 3 g, Carbohydrates 9 g, Fat 1 g, Sodium 129 mg

Whole Grain Pancakes

Yield: 8 (4-inch) pancakes

 powerhouse of a pancake, this recipe can be made wheat-free by substituting any other flour for the wheat, such as barley, buckwheat, rice, or oat.

¼ cup unbleached flour

¼ cup whole wheat flour

¼ cup cornmeal

2 scoops GeniSoy Natural Protein Powder or GeniSoy Natural Vanilla Shake Powder (½ cup)

2 teaspoons non-aluminum baking powder

¼ teaspoon salt

1⅓ cups soymilk or water

2 tablespoons oil

Mix the dry ingredients together. Pour in the soymilk or water and oil, and stir just until moistened. Spoon onto a hot griddle, and spread slightly with the spoon if necessary. Cook on both sides until browned.

Per pancake: Calories 110, Total Protein 8 g, Soy Protein 7 g, Carbohydrates 10 g, Fat 4 g, Sodium 144 mg

Crêpes

Yield: 6 (10-inch) crêpes

Stir the dry ingredients together in a bowl. Pour in the soymilk and whip. Add 1½ teaspoons of the oil to a hot non-stick crêpe pan, then roll and turn the pan to cover it with the oil.

Pour in ½ cup of the crêpe batter, and immediately roll and turn the pan so it is evenly covered with the batter. Cook over medium-high heat until the crêpe starts to bubble and pull away from the sides of the pan. Carefully loosen the crêpe at the edges, and flip over to cook the other side until it shows flecks of golden color.

Prepare the remaining crêpe batter the same way. Serve hot.

Dry Ingredients

1½ scoops GeniSoy Natural Protein Powder (6 tablespoons)

6 tablespoons unbleached flour

3 tablespoons nutritional yeast flakes

¼ teaspoon salt

Liquid Ingredients

2 cups plain soymilk

1 tablespoon oil

Per crêpe: Calories 109, Total Protein 11 g, Soy Protein 8 g, Carbohydrates 8 g, Fat 3 g, Sodium 176 mg

Orange-Apricot Oatmeal

Yield: 2 servings

chewy and satisfying hot cereal, with just a hint of sweetness. Dried apricots are an excellent source of vitamin A, iron, and potassium. Seek out organic dried apricots; they will be a deep orange-brown color. Avoid ones that are bright orange because they will have been treated with sulfur dioxide.

1 cup old-fashioned rolled oats

1¼ cups cold water

½ cup orange juice

2 tablespoons chopped dried apricots

¼ teaspoon nutmeg

2 tablespoons GeniSoy Natural Protein Powder

Tiny pinch of salt

Flavoring options

Sweetener of your choice

2 teaspoons organic flax oil

2 tablespoons chopped walnuts, almonds, or pecans, raw or lightly pan-toasted

Combine all the ingredients, except the protein powder and flavoring options, in a medium saucepan, and bring to a boil. Cover and reduce the heat to low. Simmer 5 minutes, stirring once or twice.

Remove from the heat, add the protein powder, cover, and let sit for 2 to 5 minutes.

Stir in the sweetener and flax oil, if using. Sprinkle 1 tablespoon nuts over each serving, if desired.

Tip: To pan-toast the nuts, lightly roast them in a dry skillet over medium heat, stirring often, until fragrant and golden brown.

Per serving: Calories 239, Total Protein 14 g, Soy Protein 6 g, Carbohydrates 38 g, Fat 3 g, Sodium 74 mg

Cinnamon-Apple Oatmeal

Yield: 2 servings

Old-fashioned rolled oats make a hearty morning meal. If you prefer, use dates or raisins instead of, or in addition to, the dried apples.

Combine all the ingredients, except the protein powder and flavoring options, in a medium saucepan, and bring to a boil. Cover and reduce the heat to low. Simmer 5 minutes, stirring once or twice.

Remove from the heat, add the protein powder, cover, and let sit for 2 to 5 minutes.

Stir in the sweetener and flax oil, if using. Sprinkle 1 tablespoon nuts over each serving, if desired.

1 cup old-fashioned rolled oats

1¼ cups cold water

½ cup apple juice

2 tablespoons chopped dried apples

¼ teaspoon cinnamon

Tiny pinch of salt

2 tablespoons GeniSoy Natural Protein Powder

Flavoring options

Sweetener of your choice

2 teaspoons organic flax oil

2 tablespoons chopped walnuts, almonds, or pecans, raw or lightly pan toasted

Per serving: Calories 261, Total Protein 14 g, Soy Protein 6 g, Carbohydrates 44 g, Fat 3 g, Sodium 75 mg

Breads and Baked Goods

THE MAGIC OF SOY

Applesauce Raisin Muffins

Yield: 12 muffins

Preheat the oven to 350°F.

Mix the liquid ingredients in a mixing bowl.

Sift the dry ingredients into the liquid ingredients. Stir well but don't overbeat.

Add the raisins and mix them in just before spooning the muffins into lightly oiled muffin tins. Bake for 15 to 18 minutes.

Test the muffins by inserting a toothpick in the middle of a muffin. If the toothpick comes out clean, the muffins are done.

Liquid Ingredients

1 cup applesauce

1 cup orange juice

2 tablespoons oil

2 tablespoons liquid sweetener

1 tablespoon brown sugar

Dry Ingredients

1¾ cups flour

2½ scoops GeniSoy Natural Protein Powder (½ cup plus 2 tablespoons)

1½ teaspoons baking soda

1 teaspoon cinnamon

¼ teaspoon salt

½ cup raisins

Per muffin: Calories 149, Total Protein 7 g, Soy Protein 5 g, Carbohydrates 24 g, Fat 2 g, Sodium 108 mg

Blueberry Soy Muffins

Yield: 12 muffins

ake these sweet, hearty muffins with either fresh or frozen blueberries. These muffins freeze well.

Dry Ingredients

2 cups whole wheat pastry flour

1 scoop GeniSoy Natural Vanilla Shake Powder (¼ cup)

½ cup sugar

1 tablespoon non-aluminum baking powder

½ teaspoon salt

Liquid Ingredients

1½ cups soymilk

¼ cup canola oil

1 cup fresh or frozen blueberries

Preheat the oven to 400°F.

Mix the dry ingredients together, and make a well in the middle.

Whip together the soymilk and oil. Pour into the well in the dry ingredients, and stir just until blended. Fold in the blueberries, pour into oiled muffin tins, and bake for about 20 minutes until browned.

Per muffin: Calories 164, Total Protein 5 g, Soy Protein 2 g, Carbohydrates 25 g, Fat 5 g, Sodium 110 mg

Tomato Herb Muffins

Yield: 12 *muffins*

Preheat the oven to 350°F.

In a mixing bowl, stir the tomato purée, rolled oats, rosemary, and thyme, and let rest for 10 minutes to soften the rolled oats and herbs.

Add the oil and molasses to the bowl of tomato ingredients.

Sift the flour, cornmeal, protein powder, baking powder, and salt into the liquid ingredients, and mix. Fill lightly oiled muffin tins to the top, and bake for 20 minutes.

Test to see if the muffins are done by inserting a toothpick in the middle of a muffin. If the toothpick comes out clean, the muffins are done.

2½ cups tomato purée (4 medium tomatoes, blended)

1 cup rolled oats

1 teaspoon crushed rosemary

½ teaspoon thyme

3 tablespoons canola oil

3 tablespoons molasses

1½ cups unbleached white flour

¾ cup cornmeal

2½ scoops GeniSoy Natural Protein Powder (½ cup plus 2 tablespoons)

3 teaspoons non-aluminum baking powder

½ teaspoon salt

Per muffin: Calories 199, Total Protein 9 g, Soy Protein 5 g, Carbohydrates 31 g, Fat 3 g, Sodium 177 mg

Corn Muffins

Yield: 12 muffins

Dry Ingredients

1½ cups cornmeal

1¼ cups unbleached flour

1 scoop GeniSoy Natural Protein Powder (¼ cup)

1 teaspoon salt

1 tablespoon non-aluminum baking powder

2 tablespoons sweetener

Dry Ingredients

¼ cup oil

2 cups soymilk

Preheat the oven to 400°F.

Mix the dry ingredients together in a bowl. Pour the oil and soymilk into the dry ingredients, and mix just until moistened.

Pour into oiled muffin tins, and bake for 20 to 25 minutes until browned.

Per muffin: Calories 177, Total Protein 6 g, Soy Protein 3 g, Carbohydrates 26 g, Fat 5 g, Sodium 207 mg

Sour Cream Streusel Coffee Cake

Yield: 1 *coffee cake* (9 to 12 *servings*)

No eggs, no milk, no butter—just pure, sweet indulgence. This is a superb cake to serve for a leisurely Sunday morning breakfast or for a special brunch or social gathering.

Preheat the oven to 350°F.

Mist an 8 x 8 x 2-inch square baking pan with nonstick cooking spray, and set it aside.

Place the ingredients for the streusel in a small bowl, and stir them together. Set aside.

Place all the wet ingredients in a large mixing bowl, and stir them together until they are well blended.

Place the dry ingredients in a medium mixing bowl, and stir them together. Gradually mix the dry ingredients into the wet ingredients, sprinkling in about ⅓ of the dry ingredients at a time. Beat well after each addition. The batter will be very thick.

Spread half of this batter evenly into the prepared pan. Sprinkle half of the reserved streusel evenly over the batter. Spread

Streusel

½ cup brown sugar

½ cup finely chopped walnuts or almonds

½ teaspoon ground cinnamon

Wet Ingredients

½ cup crumbled firm silken tofu

1 cup applesauce

⅓ cup pure maple syrup

3 tablespoons canola oil

1 teaspoon fresh lemon juice

1 teaspoon apple cider vinegar

1 teaspoon vanilla extract

Dry Ingredients

1½ cups whole wheat pastry flour

2 scoops GeniSoy Natural Protein Powder (½ cup)

1 teaspoon sugar

1 teaspoon non-aluminum baking powder

1 teaspoon baking soda

1 teaspoon salt

¼ teaspoon ground nutmeg

the remaining batter evenly over the streusel. The easiest way to do this is to place dollops of the batter on top of the streusel, and smooth it out carefully with a rubber spatula. Then sprinkle the remaining half of the streusel evenly over the top of the batter. Pat the streusel down very lightly.

Bake the coffee cake for 30 minutes, or until a cake tester inserted in the center comes out clean. Place the cake on a wire rack to cool for at least 15 minutes. Serve warm or at room temperature. Cover leftover cake tightly with plastic wrap, and store it for a day at room temperature or in the refrigerator for longer storage.

Per serving: Calories 229, Total Protein 9 g, Soy Protein 6 g, Carbohydrates 16 g, Fat 8 g, Sodium 283 mg

Cinnamon Sticky Buns

Yield: 32 rolls

Make this dough the night before and store in the refrigerator overnight. It'll be ready to shape into buns the next morning.

In a large bowl, mix the warm water and yeast. When the yeast has dissolved, add the wheat germ, protein powder, sweetener, lemon juice, salt, and turmeric. Mix in the flour and knead well for 5 to 10 minutes, using as little flour as possible. The dough should be soft and a bit sticky.

Place in an oiled bowl, and let rise overnight in the refrigerator. (This dough handles best when cold.)

Preheat the oven to 350°F.

Divide the dough in half, and roll each half into a 12 x 18-inch rectangle. Spread each rectangle with half the softened margarine and half the cinnamon. Roll up lengthwise and seal the long edge well. Cut each roll into 1-inch slices with a sharp knife. Spread ½ cup of the maple syrup in each of two 9 x 13-inch baking pans. Place the slices cut side down in the syrup, and let rise until doubled.

Bake for 20 to 25 minutes. Once out of the oven, place cookie sheets over the baking pans and flip the pans over quickly. Leave the inverted pans over the rolls so the syrup will soak into the buns as they cool.

2 cups warm water

1 package baking yeast

½ cup wheat germ

1 scoop GeniSoy Natural Protein Powder (¼ cup)

½ cup sweetener

1 tablespoon lemon juice

2 teaspoons salt

¼ teaspoon turmeric (optional, for golden color)

5 cups unbleached flour

4 tablespoons softened margarine

1 tablespoon cinnamon

1 cup maple syrup

Per bun: Calories 122, Total Protein 3 g, Soy Protein 1 g, Carbohydrates 23 g, Fat 2 g, Sodium 160 mg

Banana Tea Loaf

Yield: 1 *loaf* (10 *to* 12 *servings*)

1¾ cups whole wheat pastry flour

3 scoops Plain or GeniSoy Natural Vanilla Shake Powder (¾ cup)

2 teaspoons non-aluminum baking powder (such as Rumford)

1 teaspoon baking soda

1½ cups mashed, ripe bananas (about 3 to 4 medium)

6 tablespoons apple juice concentrate

2 tablespoons corn oil or canola oil

2 teaspoons vanilla extract

⅓ cup chopped walnuts

⅓ cup raisins or currants (optional)

Preheat the oven to 350°F.

Mist an 8½ x 4½-inch loaf pan with nonstick cooking spray, and set it aside.

Place the flour, protein powder, baking powder, and baking soda in a large mixing bowl, and stir them together.

In a medium mixing bowl, place the mashed banana, apple juice concentrate, oil, and vanilla. Stir them together until they are well combined. Pour this liquid mixture into the flour mixture, and stir them together to form a very thick batter. Stir in the walnuts and raisins or currants.

Spoon the batter into the loaf pan, place on the center rack of the oven, and bake for about 50 minutes, or until a cake tester inserted in the center tests clean.

Remove the bread from the oven. Turn it out of the loaf pan onto a cooling rack, and carefully turn the bread upright. Allow the bread to cool completely before slicing or storing it. Wrap the cooled bread tightly. Store in the refrigerator for up to 7 days.

Per serving: Calories 179, Total Protein 10 g, Soy Protein 7 g, Carbohydrates 24 g, Fat 4 g, Sodium 81 mg

Cranberry Nut Bread

Yield: 2 loaves (16 slices)

Preheat the oven to 350°F.

Combine the flour, baking powder, baking soda, and salt in a bowl, and mix together. With a mixer, beat together the tofu, brown sugar, oil, vanilla, and protein powder.

Add the flour mixture and beat in until blended.

Add the cranberries and walnuts, and beat again briefly until blended.

Divide the batter evenly between 2 oiled loaf pans, and bake for about 50 to 60 minutes.

2½ cups unbleached or half whole wheat flour

1 teaspoon non-aluminum baking powder

½ teaspoon baking soda

½ teaspoon salt

1 (12.3-ounce) package firm silken tofu

1 cup brown sugar

½ cup oil

2 teaspoons vanilla

2 scoops GeniSoy Natural Vanilla Shake Powder (½ cup)

1 cup fresh cranberries

½ cup chopped walnuts

Per slice: Calories 213, Total Protein 6 g, Soy Protein 3 g, Carbohydrates 26 g, Fat 10 g, Sodium 100 mg

Quick Soy Biscuits

Yield: 6 to 8 biscuits

Dry Ingredients

1¾ cups flour

1½ scoops GeniSoy Natural Protein Powder (¼ cup plus 2 tablespoons)

1 tablespoon non-aluminum baking powder

½ teaspoon salt

Liquid Ingredients

¾ cup soymilk or soy yogurt

¼ cup canola or soy oil

Preheat the oven to 400°F.

Mix the dry ingredients together in a bowl. Mix the soymilk or soy yogurt and oil in a cup, and pour into the dry ingredients. Mix together with as few strokes a possible.

Roll out on a floured board, and cut into biscuits, or drop onto a baking sheet by spoonfuls. Bake for 12 to 15 minutes, or until browned.

Per biscuit: Calories 198, Total Protein 9 g, Soy Protein 6 g, Carbohydrates 22 g, Fat 9 g, Sodium 218 mg

Pizza Crust

Yield: One 12-inch crust (4 to 6 servings)

Dissolve the active dry yeast in the warm water, and let it stand for about 5 minutes until it starts foaming.

In a mixing bowl, stir the sweetener and olive oil into the dissolved yeast, then beat and knead in the rest of the ingredients until the dough is smooth and elastic. Cover and let the dough rise in a warm place until almost doubled in bulk.

Preheat the oven to 500°F.

Punch down the dough and roll or stretch it to fit a 12-inch pizza pan that has been sprinkled with cornmeal. Spread your favorite pizza toppings over the dough, and bake until browned and bubbling.

1 tablespoon active dry yeast

1 cup warm water

1 tablespoon sweetener

1 tablespoon olive oil

1 teaspoon salt

1 cup unbleached flour

2 scoops GeniSoy Natural Protein Powder (½ cup)

½ cup whole wheat flour

Per serving: Calories 202, Total Protein 14 g, Soy Protein 10 g, Carbohydrates 26 g, Fat 2 g, Sodium 544 mg

Focaccia

Yield: 8 slices

1 tablespoon active dry yeast

1¼ cups warm water

1 tablespoon sweetener of choice

1 tablespoon olive oil

1 teaspoon salt

1½ cups whole wheat pastry flour

1 cup unbleached white flour

2 scoops GeniSoy Natural Protein Powder (½ cup)

½ cup seeded and chopped plum tomatoes

1 tablespoon finely chopped fresh basil

¼ cup finely chopped onions

1 clove garlic, finely minced

½ cup sliced or chopped olives

Sprinkle the yeast over the warm water, and let it soften and dissolve for about 5 minutes.

Beat in the sweetener, olive oil, and salt with a heavy duty mixer or wooden spoon. Add the whole wheat pastry flour, and beat until the dough is smooth and elastic. Add the unbleached flour and protein powder, and beat and knead until smooth and elastic. Cover the dough in a lightly oiled bowl, and let it rise in a warm place until double in bulk.

Preheat the oven to 450°F.

Punch down the dough and knead briefly. Lightly oil a 12-inch round pizza pan. Roll and stretch the dough to fit the pan. Punch holes in the dough about every inch over the pan with the end of a wooden spoon or chopstick.

Sprinkle the tomatoes, basil, onions, garlic, and olives over the top. Let rise again about 15 minutes. Bake for about 12 minutes, or until browned. Cut into wedges and serve.

Per slice: Calories 193, Total Protein 11 g, Soy Protein 6 g, Carbohydrates 28 g, Fat 5 g, Sodium 406 mg

Wheat Tortillas

Yield: 6 to 8 (8-inch) tortillas

These tortillas will roll out easily with no extra flour needed.

In a food processor, mix together the dry ingredients. Mix the liquid ingredients together, and pour into the processor while it is running. Process until the dough forms a ball.

Separate the dough into 8 balls, and roll out into 8-inch rounds. Cook each tortilla on a hot griddle on both sides until it bubbles up, making golden brown spots all over. Store inside a towel while cooking the remaining tortillas, and serve hot.

Dry Ingredients

1 cup unbleached flour

½ cup whole wheat flour

2 scoops GeniSoy Natural Protein Powder (½ cup)

½ teaspoon salt

Liquid Ingredients

¾ cup water

2 tablespoons oil

Per tortilla: Calories 149, Total Protein 10 g, Soy Protein 7 g, Carbohydrates 18 g, Fat 3 g, Sodium 236 mg

Crackers

Yield: One 11 x 17-inch cookie sheet (Forty 2-inch squares)

Crispy crackers are a good addition to any soup. Great for dunking.

2 cups unbleached white flour

2 scoops GeniSoy Natural Protein Powder (½ cup)

½ cup nutritional yeast flakes

1 tablespoon sesame seeds

1 teaspoon garlic powder

1 teaspoon chili powder

½ teaspoon salt

⅔ cup water

3 tablespoons soy sauce

3 tablespoons oil

Preheat the oven to 375°F.

Mix the flour, protein powder, nutritional yeast, sesame seeds, garlic, chili powder, and salt in a mixing bowl.

Make a hole in the center of the dry ingredients, add the water, soy sauce, and oil, and stir well. You should have a stiff but workable dough. Add more water if the dough is too stiff.

Press into a cookie sheet, working out from the center, until the dough evenly covers the whole sheet. You can use a rolling pin to help. Pat down the dough so the top is smooth, and cut into 2-inch square pieces. Poke a fork in the center of each cracker to prevent it from bubbling up. Bake for 15 minutes, or until golden brown. These crackers will be soft when warm but will get crispy as they cool.

Per 4 crackers: Calories165 , Total Protein 10 g, Soy Protein 5 g, Carbohydrates 20 g, Fat 5 g, Sodium 474 mg

Cheezy Bread Sticks

Yield: 3 dozen bread sticks

lthough great with any meal, these delicious bread sticks are ideal with soups and salads and have a great "cheese" flavor.

Place the yeast and sugar in a large mixing bowl. Add the warm water, and let the mixture rest for about 10 minutes until it is foamy. Then stir in the oil.

Stir in the nutritional yeast flakes, protein powder, salt, garlic granules, and pepper, and mix well. Then gradually beat in the 3 cups of flour (more or less, as needed) with a wooden spoon, adding only ½ cup at a time, until the mixture forms a soft but kneadable dough.

Turn the dough out onto a floured board, and knead it for 5 minutes until it is smooth and elastic, adding more flour as necessary. Alternatively, knead the dough directly in the mixing bowl.

Lightly oil a clean, large mixing bowl, and place the dough in it. Turn the dough around so that it is lightly oiled all over. Cover the bowl with a clean, damp tea

1½ tablespoons active dry baking yeast

2 tablespoons unbleached cane sugar or other sweetener of your choice

1½ cups warm water (110°F to 115°F)

¼ cup olive oil

½ cup nutritional yeast flakes

2 scoops GeniSoy Natural Protein Powder (½ cup)

1 teaspoon salt

½ teaspoon garlic granules

Pinch of ground black pepper

Approximately 3 cups whole wheat bread flour, more or less as needed, or half unbleached white flour and half whole wheat flour

Sesame or poppy seeds, as needed (optional)

towel, and let the dough rise in a warm place for about 60 minutes, or until doubled in size.

Preheat the oven to 400°F.

Mist two baking sheets with non-stick cooking spray, and set them aside.

Punch the dough straight down into the center. Then punch it in about 8 places. Knead the dough briefly, then slice it into quarters. Working with one of the quarters at a time, cut it into 9 equal pieces. Keep the remaining dough covered with plastic wrap or a lightly dampened tea towel. Shape each piece into a pencil-size stick by rolling it between the palms of your hands or between the palm of one hand and a bread board or countertop. If desired, roll it in sesame or poppy seeds. Place the bread sticks as they are formed onto the prepared baking sheets.

Using the center rack of the oven, bake one sheet of bread sticks at a time for about 10 minutes, or until they are golden brown. Keep the remaining sheet of bread sticks covered with plastic wrap or a lightly dampened tea towel. Transfer the baked bread sticks to a cooling rack, and bake the second batch in the same fashion. Serve warm or at room temperature.

Per 2 sticks: Calories 122, Total Protein 7 g, Soy Protein 3 g, Carbohydrates 16 g, Fat 2 g, Sodium 157 mg

Bagels

Yield: 12 large bagels

agels are easy and fun to make. These bagels are chewy and lend themselves to various accompaniments. A combination of sliced tofu, avocado, pesto, and sprouts is our favorite, but fruit jams and creamy spreads are good too.

In a medium mixing bowl, combine the lukewarm water, liquid sweetener, yeast, and 1½ cups unbleached flour to form a sponge which will bubble up. Let set undisturbed for 10 to 15 minutes.

While the sponge is forming, fill a pot which is at least 9 inches wide with 3 to 4 quarts of water to a depth of 3½ to 4 inches, and bring to a boil.

Preheat the oven to 350°F.

Add the salt, protein powder, whole wheat flour, and remaining white flour to the sponge mixture after it has become foamy. Mix well with a wooden spoon, then turn onto a lightly floured counter, and knead for 5 to 10 minutes. The dough will become smooth and satiny. Only add more flour if it is sticking to your hands. The dough should be soft, not stiff.

3 cups lukewarm water

3 tablespoons liquid sweetener

1 tablespoon active dry yeast

2 cups unbleached white flour

1 teaspoon salt

2½ scoops GeniSoy Natural Protein Powder (½ cup plus 2 tablespoons)

1 cup whole wheat flour

3 to 4 cups unbleached white flour

Sesame seeds, for topping (optional)

Poppy seeds, for topping (optional)

Divide the dough into 12 balls. To form the bagels, take each ball and roll it firmly on the counter, pressing down and using the palm of your hand to make a smooth ball. Pick up the ball, press your thumb through the center, and stretch the dough out from the center all around to form a bagel shape. The hole should be about 1 inch across. Set each bagel on a lightly floured surface, and make the next one. Let the bagels rest for 10 to 15 minutes to rise. Lightly sprinkle a baking sheet with cornmeal or oil.

Drop each bagel, in the order that you made them, into a pot of boiling water. Cook 4 at once. Cook for 2½ minutes on one side, then turn over with a slotted spoon, and cook 2½ minutes on the other side. With the slotted spoon, remove a bagel, and place it on the prepared baking sheet with the top side up. Sometimes the bagels turn over during boiling so the flat bottom side (which is sometimes cracked) ends up on top after you've turned them over. Be sure to put that side down on the baking sheet. If you would like to sprinkle the tops with sesame seeds or poppy seeds, do this right after they are removed from the boiling water.

Boil a second batch and put 2 bagels on the first baking sheet. You will have 1 sheet of 6 bagels ready to bake, and 2 more bagels on the next sheet waiting for the next 4 bagels to boil.

Start baking the first batch as soon as the first 6 are boiled; don't wait for the next batch to finish boiling. Bake for 20 minutes. You may need to turn the sheet around in the oven half way through baking if your oven doesn't bake evenly. When the bagels are done, remove from the sheets, place in a large bowl, and cover with a clean dish cloth to keep the bagels soft.

Per bagel: Calories 254, Total Protein 12 g, Soy Protein 5 g, Carbohydrates 50 g, Fat 0 g, Sodium 239 mg

Challah

Yield: 16 slices

In a large mixing bowl, combine the water and yeast. When the yeast has dissolved, add the mashed potatoes, protein powder, wheat germ, sugar, lemon juice, salt, and turmeric. Mix in the flour, and knead well for 5 to 10 minutes, using as little flour as possible—the dough should be soft and a bit sticky.

Place the dough in an oiled bowl large enough to allow the dough to double. Oil the top and cover with plastic wrap. Let rise overnight or for 8 to 12 hours in the refrigerator. (The dough will handle better when cold.)

Several hours before serving, shape the dough into 2 braided loaves. Cover and let rise until doubled. Just before baking, combine the cold water and cornstarch. Brush this mixture over the braided loaves and sprinkle with sesame or poppy seeds. Bake at 350°F for about 30 minutes until nicely browned. Cook on racks.

2 cups warm water

1 package active baking yeast

½ cup leftover mashed potatoes (or ½ cup instant potato flakes mixed with ⅓ cup boiling water)

2 scoops GeniSoy Natural Protein Powder (½ cup)

½ cup wheat germ

½ cup sugar

1 tablespoon lemon juice

2 teaspoons salt

¼ teaspoon turmeric

5 cups unbleached flour

½ cup cold water

1 teaspoon cornstarch

Sesame or poppy seeds, for topping

Per slice: Calories 180, Total Protein 8 g, Soy Protein 3 g, Carbohydrates 36 g, Fat 0 g, Sodium 303 mg

Sauces, Gravies, Dips, Dressings, and Spreads

THE

MAGIC

OF SOY

Thousand Island Dressing

Yield: about ¾ cup

Thousand Island dressing used to mean "a thousand calories and fat grams." No longer! Indulge your senses with this thick and luxurious, but healthful, low-fat temptation.

Combine all the ingredients in a blender or food processor fitted with a metal blade, and process until creamy.

½ cup crumbled silken tofu

2 tablespoons ketchup

2 tablespoons GeniSoy Natural Protein Powder

1½ tablespoons pickle relish, lightly drained

1 tablespoon extra-virgin olive oil

1 tablespoon fresh lemon juice

1 tablespoon chopped onions, or ½ teaspoon onion powder

Pinch of salt

Per 2 tablespoons: Calories 54, Total Protein 4 g, Soy Protein 4 g, Carbohydrates 4 g, Fat 3 g, Sodium 111 mg

Classic Ranch Dressing

Yield: about ¾ cup

¾ cup crumbled silken tofu

2 tablespoons GeniSoy Natural Protein Powder

2 tablespoons extra-virgin olive oil

1 tablespoon umeboshi plum vinegar

1 tablespoon fresh lemon juice

1 tablespoon water

½ teaspoon tarragon

¼ teaspoon dill

¼ teaspoon crushed garlic

Pinch of dry mustard

Combine all the ingredients in a blender or food processor, and process until smooth and creamy.

Per 2 tablespoons: Calories 72, Total Protein 5 g, Soy Protein 5 g, Carbohydrates 1 g, Fat 5 g, Sodium 37 mg

Cole Slaw Dressing

Yield: about 1½ cups (enough for 9 to 10 cups shredded vegetables)

1 clove garlic, minced

½ cup olive oil

½ cup apple cider vinegar

¼ cup sweetener of choice

1 scoop GeniSoy Natural Protein Powder (¼ cup)

1 tablespoon miso, or 1 teaspoon salt

1 very small onion, or ¼ medium onion, chopped

Process all the ingredients together in a blender, and chill in the refrigerator until ready to use.

Per 2 tablespoons: Calories 115, Total Protein 2 g, Soy Protein 2 g, Carbohydrates 6 g, Fat 9 g, Sodium 25 mg

Low-Fat Egg-Free Mayonnaise

Yield: about 1⅓ cups

Mayonnaise has a reputation for being ultra-high in fat as well as delicious. Try this tasty egg-free version, and indulge to your heart's content.

Place all the ingredients in a blender or food processor fitted with a metal blade, and process several minutes until the mixture is very smooth and creamy.

Use at once, or transfer the mayonnaise to a storage container, and chill it in the refrigerator. It should keep for about a week.

1½ cups crumbled firm silken tofu

2 tablespoons GeniSoy Natural Protein Powder

2 tablespoons canola oil or olive oil

2 teaspoons fresh lemon juice

2 teaspoons apple cider vinegar

2 teaspoons nutritional yeast flakes

1 to 2 teaspoons sweetener of your choice

Heaping ½ teaspoon salt

½ teaspoon prepared yellow mustard

Per tablespoon: Calories 29, Total Protein 2 g, Soy Protein 2 g, Carbohydrates 1 g, Fat 2 g, Sodium 68 mg

Tofu Sour Cream

Yield: about 1¼ cups

 ppropriately tart, creamy, and delicious, Tofu Sour Cream is the ideal nondairy replacement for its dairy counterpart.

1½ cups crumbled firm silken tofu

2 tablespoons GeniSoy Natural Protein Powder

1 tablespoon canola oil

2 teaspoons nutritional yeast flakes

2 teaspoons fresh lemon juice

2 teaspoons apple cider vinegar

1 teaspoon sweetener of your choice

½ teaspoon salt

Place all the ingredients in a blender or a food processor fitted with a metal blade. Process several minutes until the mixture is very smooth and creamy.

Transfer the mixture to a storage container, and store it in the refrigerator. It will keep for about 5 days.

Per 2 tablespoons: Calories 48, Total Protein 4 g, Soy Protein 4 g, Carbohydrates 2 g, Fat 3 g, Sodium 137 mg

Tofu Cream Cheeze Spread

Yield: 1 *cup*

Place the tofu in a clean tea towel, gather the end up, and twist and squeeze for a couple of minutes to extract most of the water. Crumble into a mixing bowl, and mix in the remaining ingredients. Process in 2 batches in a blender or all at once in a food processor for several minutes until the mixture is very smooth. (You may have to stop the machine and loosen the mixture with a spatula once or twice.) Use right away or scrape it into a covered container and refrigerate. It firms up with refrigeration.

1 (12.3-ounce) box extra-firm silken tofu

3½ tablespoons cashew or almond butter, or tahini

2 tablespoons GeniSoy Natural Protein Powder

5 teaspoons lemon juice

½ teaspoon salt

1 teaspoon liquid sweetener (optional)

Per 2 tablespoons: Calories 75, Total Protein 6 g, Soy Protein 4 g, Carbohydrates 3 g, Fat 5 g, Sodium 167 mg

Rich Brown Gravy

Yield: about 1⅓ cups (4 servings)

This gravy will introduce you to dark miso, if you're not already familiar with it. It is a salty, dark brown paste with a lightly tangy bite, similar to mild cheese. Popular in Japan for its hearty flavor and health-giving properties, it's the perfect ingredient for making brown gravy easily and quickly.

2 tablespoons dark miso

2 tablespoons flour

2 tablespoons GeniSoy Natural Protein Powder

2 tablespoons water

1 cup water

Blend the miso, flour, protein powder, and 2 tablespoons of the water together into a smooth paste. Gradually add half the remaining water with a wire whisk, a little at a time, then whisk in the rest of the water. Simmer on top of the stove in a saucepan, stirring constantly until thick, or microwave for 3 minutes on full power. (Stop and whisk halfway through cooking.)

Per serving: Calories 43, Total Protein 4 g, Soy Protein 4 g, Carbohydrates 5 g, Fat 0 g, Sodium 36 mg

Nondairy Bechamel

Yield: 2 cups

I think this recipe is a great improvement upon vegan white sauces made completely with soymilk, which I find too sweet. The tofu and broth cube add richness without much fat. This rich-tasting sauce, used frequently in Italian cooking, is actually quite low in fat. It is a key ingredient in dishes such as lasagne. It can be used as an all-purpose white sauce in all of your cooking and as a topping for Greek dishes, such as vegetarian moussaka.

Place the soymilk, tofu, water, protein powder, broth cube or powder, and salt in a blender, and mix until very smooth. Set aside.

In a medium, heavy saucepan over medium-high heat, heat the oil and whisk in 1½ tablespoons of flour, adding more if necessary to make the mixture thicker. Whisk for a few minutes, but remove from the heat just before it starts to change color. (You want a white roux.)

Add to the soymilk mixture in the blender, and process for a few seconds. Pour the mixture back into the saucepan. Cook over medium-high heat, stirring frequently, until the sauce thickens and boils. Reduce the temperature to low, and simmer for a few minutes to cook thoroughly. Whisk in the nutmeg and pepper.

1½ cups soymilk

½ cup crumbled extra-firm silken tofu or medium-firm regular tofu

½ cup water

1 scoop GeniSoy Natural Protein Powder (¼ cup)

1 chicken-style vegetarian broth cube, crumbled, or enough broth powder to flavor 1 cup liquid

½ teaspoon salt

2 tablespoons nondairy margarine or extra-virgin olive oil

1½ to 3 tablespoons unbleached flour

Large pinch each of freshly grated nutmeg and white pepper

Microwave Option

Using a large microwave-safe
bowl, heat the oil in the
microwave on high for 45 seconds. Whisk in the flour and
microwave on high for 2 minutes. Add to the soymilk mixture in the blender, and process
briefly, then pour the mixture
back into the bowl. Microwave
on high for 2 minutes. Whisk.
Microwave for 2 more minutes,
then whisk again. Microwave
for 2 minutes more, and whisk
in the nutmeg and pepper.

*Per ½ cup: Calories 154, Total Protein 11 g, Soy Protein 11 g,
Carbohydrates 6 g, Fat 9 g, Sodium 436 mg*

Hollandaze Sauce

Yield: 2 cups

This rich, creamy, lemony sauce will remind you of hollandaise, without missing the butter or eggs. It's wonderful and festive over steamed broccoli or baked potatoes. The sauce may be made ahead of time and refrigerated. Heat it gently according to the recipe directions before serving. Courtesy of Mark Shadle and Lisa Magee, owners of It's Only Natural Restaurant, an extraordinary, totally vegan eatery in Middletown, Connecticut.

Place all the ingredients, except the olive oil, in a blender or food processor, and process until very smooth and creamy. Drizzle in the olive oil while continuing to blend.

Transfer the sauce to a 1-quart saucepan, and place it over medium-low heat. Warm the sauce, stirring often, until it is heated through. Do not boil!

1½ cups crumbled firm silken tofu

½ cup soymilk

3 tablespoons GeniSoy Natural Protein Powder

1 tablespoon fresh lemon juice

1 tablespoon nutritional yeast flakes

1 tablespoon tahini

1 teaspoon turmeric (for a buttery-yellow color)

½ teaspoon dried tarragon leaves

¼ cup olive oil

Per ¼ cup: Calories 122, Total Protein 7 g, Soy Protein 6 g, Carbohydrates 3 g, Fat 9 g, Sodium 50 mg

Velvety Cheeze Sauce

Yield: about 2 cups

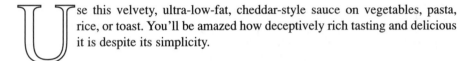se this velvety, ultra-low-fat, cheddar-style sauce on vegetables, pasta, rice, or toast. You'll be amazed how deceptively rich tasting and delicious it is despite its simplicity.

1 medium potato, peeled and coarsely chopped

¾ cup water

½ cup chopped carrots

½ cup chopped onions

½ to 1 teaspoon crushed garlic

¾ cup crumbled silken tofu

1 scoop GeniSoy Natural Protein Powder (¼ cup)

½ cup nutritional yeast flakes

1 tablespoon fresh lemon juice

1 teaspoon salt

Place the potato, water, carrots, onions, and garlic in a medium saucepan, and bring to a boil. Reduce the heat to medium, cover, and simmer, stirring once or twice, until the vegetables are tender, about 10 minutes.

Transfer the cooked vegetables, their cooking liquid, and the remaining ingredients to a blender, and purée in batches into a completely smooth sauce.

Rinse out the saucepan and return the blended mixture to it. Warm the sauce over low heat, stirring often until hot.

Per ½ cup: Calories 154, Total Protein 16 g, Soy Protein 10 g, Carbohydrates 18 g, Fat 2 g, Sodium 660 mg

Melty Soy Pizza Cheese

Yield: *about 1¼ cups*

This easy recipe is tastier than commercial vegan cheese substitutes—and cheaper. Drizzle it hot over pizza or casseroles before baking. It's most appealing if you also run it briefly under the broiler after baking, just enough to make it really bubbly, with a thin crust on top.

Place the soymilk, nutritional yeast, cornstarch, flour, protein powder, lemon juice, salt, and garlic granules in a blender, and process until smooth. Pour the mixture into a small saucepan. Stir over medium heat until it starts to thicken, then let bubble 30 seconds and whisk vigorously.

Microwave Option

Pour the mixture into a medium microwave-proof bowl. Microwave on high for 2 minutes, whisk, then microwave at 50 percent (or medium) power for 2 minutes, and whisk again.

Whisk in the water and oil. Drizzle immediately over pizza or other food, and bake or broil until a skin forms on top. Or refrigerate for up to a week. It will get quite firm upon chilling but will still be spreadable. You can spread the firm cheese on bread or quesadillas for grilling, or heat to thin it out for pouring over food.

1 cup soymilk

¼ cup nutritional yeast flakes

2 tablespoons cornstarch

1 tablespoon white flour

2 tablespoons GeniSoy Natural Protein Powder

1 teaspoon lemon juice

½ teaspoon salt

¼ teaspoon garlic granules

2 tablespoons water

1 to 2 tablespoons canola oil or other neutral-tasting vegetable oil

Per ¼ cup: Calories 99, Total Protein 6 g, Soy Protein 4 g, Carbohydrates 7 g, Fat 5 g, Sodium 256 mg

Spicy Bean Dip or "Refried" Beans

Yield: 3½ to 4 cups

This fat-free dip gets its light texture from being whirled for several minutes in the food processor. It can be made with black, red, or pinto beans, pinto or black bean flakes, or, in a pinch, red lentils cooked for 10 minutes. Good hot or cold, it makes a great stand-in for refried beans.

3 (15-ounce) cans, or 4½ cups cooked plain beans, drained

2 scoops GeniSoy Natural Protein Powder (½ cup)

1 small onion, minced

2 tablespoons cider vinegar or wine vinegar

1 teaspoon salt

1 teaspoon ground cumin

1 teaspoon dried oregano

3 cloves garlic, crushed, or 1 teaspoon garlic granules

1 teaspoon chile powder with hot red pepper sauce to taste and a few dashes of liquid smoke, or 2 teaspoons chipotle chile

Place all the ingredients in a food processor, and blend for several minutes until very smooth.

Place in a serving bowl, cover, and refrigerate. If you like, heat the dip in the microwave on high for about 3 minutes or in a skillet (stirring constantly) until heated through. Serve with baked tortilla chips.

Per ¼ cup: Calories 134, Total Protein 9 g, Soy Protein 3 g, Carbohydrates 23 g, Fat 0 g, Sodium 182 mg

Hummus

Yield: 2 cups

This is a rich spread that goes well on pita bread with sprouts and tomato. It makes great travel or picnic food—be sure to keep chilled until lunchtime.

Puree all of the ingredients together, and let them sit for at least 30 minutes before eating to let the flavors develop.

2 cups cooked garbanzo beans

2 scoops GeniSoy Natural Protein Powder (½ cup)

¼ cup bean stock leftover from cooking (or the juice left in the can if using canned beans)

¼ cup lemon juice

2 cloves garlic

2 tablespoons chopped fresh parsley

1 tablespoon soy sauce

3 tablespoons tahini

Per ¼ cup: Calories 128, Total Protein 10 g, Soy Protein 6 g, Carbohydrates 14 g, Fat 3 g, Sodium 206 mg

Chick-Pea Spread

Yield: 2 cups

Spread this savory spread on crackers or bread. It can be served as an appetizer or with soup or salad.

1 medium onion, chopped

1 red bell pepper, chopped

2 cloves garlic, minced

1 teaspoon olive oil

1 tomato, peeled and chopped (½ pound)

2 tablespoons chopped fresh parsley

2 cups cooked chick-peas, or 1 (16-ounce) can, drained

1 scoop GeniSoy Natural Protein Powder (¼ cup)

½ teaspoon salt

½ teaspoon thyme

½ teaspoon sage

Sauté the onion, bell pepper, and garlic in the olive oil. Stir in the chopped tomato at the end, and turn off the heat.

In a food processor, chop the parsley, add the sautéed vegetables, chop again, then add all the rest of the ingredients. Process until all are blended.

Per 2 tablespoons: Calories 50, Total Protein 3 g, Soy Protein 2 g, Carbohydrates 7 g, Fat 0 g, Sodium 88 mg

Italian Refried White Beans

Yield: 3 cups

Sauté the onion, bell pepper, and garlic in the olive oil. In a food processor, chop the basil, add the beans and protein powder, and process until creamy. Add all the rest of the ingredients, and process until well blended.

1 onion, chopped

1 red bell pepper, chopped

3 cloves garlic, minced

1 tablespoon olive oil

1 ounce fresh basil, chopped

2 cups cooked cannellini or great Northern beans (one 16-ounce can)

1 scoop GeniSoy Natural Protein Powder (¼ cup)

½ teaspoon salt

⅛ teaspoon freshly ground black pepper

Per 2 tablespoons: Calories 29, Total Protein 2 g, Soy Protein 1 g, Carbohydrates 4 g, Fat 0 g, Sodium 57 mg

Tofu-Miso Spread

Yield: 1¼ cups

For the best flavor, this cheesy-tasting spread needs to be made ahead of time. Spread on crackers or bread, or use as a dip for chips or vegetables.

1 clove garlic

½ pound firm tofu

2 tablespoons GeniSoy Natural Protein Powder

2 tablespoons sweet rice miso

2 tablespoons rice vinegar

2 teaspoons onion powder

Chop the garlic in a food processor. Add the rest of the ingredients, and blend until smooth. Refrigerate for a few hours or overnight for flavors to blend.

Per 2 tablespoons: Calories 30, Total Protein 3 g, Soy Protein 3 g, Carbohydrates 2 g, Fat 1 g, Sodium 16 mg

Seasoned Breading Mix

Yield: 1⅓ cups (4 servings)

This is the perfect way to add a little more protein to baked tofu, vegetable slices, or to the top of a casserole.

Mix all the ingredients together, and store in a tightly covered container in the refrigerator.

1 cup soft whole wheat bread crumbs or finely crumbled, whole grain cold cereal

¼ cup cornmeal

2 tablespoons GeniSoy Natural Protein Powder

2 teaspoons paprika

1 teaspoon salt (herbal or seasoned, if desired)

½ teaspoon black pepper

½ teaspoon ground sage

½ teaspoon dried thyme

½ teaspoon dried basil

Per serving: Calories 141, Total Protein 7 g, Soy Protein 3 g, Carbohydrates 25 g, Fat 0 g, Sodium 753 mg

Soups, Salads, and Sandwich Fillings

THE

MAGIC

OF SOY

Black Bean Soup

Yield: 6 servings

E ating black beans, dark and warming, is comforting any time of the year. With or without the scoop of rice, cornmeal muffins go well with this soup.

Soak the beans overnight; drain and rinse. In a soup pot, combine the soaked beans with the water, bay leaf, onion, and green pepper, and simmer for 1½ to 2 hours until the the beans are very soft.

Add the dissolved protein powder and water, oregano, cumin, salt, and lemon juice, and cook for 5 more minutes. Serve with a scoop of cooked rice in the middle of each bowl, if you wish, and garnish with chopped scallions.

2 cups dry black beans (1 pound)

7 cups water

1 bay leaf

1 large onion, finely chopped

1 green pepper, chopped

2 scoops GeniSoy Natural Protein Powder (½ cup) dissolved in 1 cup water

1 teaspoon oregano

2 teaspoons cumin

1 teaspoon salt

2 tablespoons lemon juice

Per serving: Calories 146, Total Protein 14 g, Soy Protein 8 g, Carbohydrates 21 g, Fat 0 g, Sodium 454 mg

Split Pea Soup

Yield: 6 servings

This soup is one of our favorites; as cold leftovers it makes a good spread on bread or crackers.

2 cups dry split peas (1 pound)

7 cups cold water

1 bay leaf

1 cup chopped onions

1 clove garlic, minced

1 cup chopped celery

2 cups cubed sweet potatoes

¼ teaspoon thyme

1½ scoops GeniSoy Natural Protein Powder (6 tablespoons) dissolved in 1 cup water

Salt and pepper, to taste

Rinse the split peas and add the cold water. Add the bay leaf, onions, garlic, celery, sweet potatoes, and thyme to the peas, and cook until the split peas are soft, about 1 to 1½ hours. Add the dissolved protein powder, water, and salt and pepper to taste.

If a smooth, creamy soup is desired, you may puree it in a food processor.

Per serving: Calories 179, Total Protein 12 g, Soy Protein 6 g, Carbohydrates 31 g, Fat 0 g, Sodium 96 mg

Corn Chowder

Yield: 11 cups

This soup is creamy and tasty and one you'll want to make again and again.

In a soup pot, cook the potatoes in the water for 5 to 10 minutes until they are soft. Then blend them in your food processor or blender, and pour the creamy liquid back into the soup pot.

In a skillet, sauté the bell pepper and onion in the oil until they are soft and start to brown. Add them to the creamy potato soup base. If you're using frozen or fresh corn, add it to the skillet of sautéed vegetables, and cook the corn briefly before adding it to the blended potato soup base.

Add the corn (if you didn't add it to the sautéed vegetables), the dissolved protein powder and soymilk, parsley, salt, and black pepper to the soup pot. Gradually return the soup to a slow boil, stirring often so it won't stick to the bottom of the pot. Simmer for several minutes. Don't sustain a rolling boil, or the milk may separate. Remove from the heat and cover until ready to serve.

4 cups chopped potatoes

2 cups water

1 bell pepper, chopped

1 onion, chopped

1 teaspoon olive oil

3 cups frozen, fresh, or canned corn (1 pound)

2 scoops GeniSoy Natural Protein Powder (½ cup) dissolved in 2 cups soymilk

½ cup chopped fresh parsley

1 teaspoon salt

⅛ teaspoon black pepper

Per 2 cups: Calories 260, Total Protein 15 g, Soy Protein 11 g, Carbohydrates 44 g, Fat 3 g, Sodium 517 mg

Creamy Mushroom Soup Deluxe

Yield: 10 *cups*

4 cups chopped potatoes

4 cups water

2 tablespoons chopped garlic

1 cup chopped green onions

1½ cups chopped celery

8 ounces fresh mushrooms, chopped

1 teaspoon olive oil

2 cups soymilk

2 scoops GeniSoy Natural Protein Powder (½ cup)

½ teaspoon salt

⅛ to ¼ teaspoon black pepper

Bring the potatoes and water to a boil, and simmer for 10 minutes until soft. Then blend them until smooth in several batches in a blender, and set aside to add to the soup later.

In a soup pot, sauté the garlic, green onions, celery, and mushrooms in the oil. Cook until the onions begin to brown and the mushrooms are soft. Stir to prevent sticking.

Add the soymilk, protein powder, salt, and black pepper to the sautéed vegetables. Stir vigorously to dissolve the protein powder into the milk. Add the blended potatoes and bring to a simmer. Cook for 2 minutes just below boiling so the milk will not separate. Turn off the heat, cover, and let sit for several minutes before serving.

Per 2 cups: Calories 209, Total Protein 15 g, Soy Protein 12 g, Carbohydrates 31 g, Fat 3 g, Sodium 380 mg

Easy Cream of Broccoli Soup

Yield: 8 to 10 cups

This soup is so satisfying and quick to make. We like to eat garlic toast with it.

In a soup pot, boil the broccoli, potatoes, and onion in the water for 10 minutes.

Add the parsley and dill to the boiling vegetables, and simmer for 5 more minutes.

In a blender or food processor, blend the contents of the soup pot along with the dissolved protein powder and soymilk in small batches. Do not overfill the blender or food processor. Put the blended soup back on the stove, and heat slowly but do not boil.

Add the salt and serve hot.

4 cups chopped broccoli (flowers, stalks, and upper stems)

3 cups cubed potatoes

1 medium onion, chopped

3 cups water

1 cup chopped parsley

½ cup chopped fresh dill

2 scoops GeniSoy Natural Protein Powder (½ cup) dissolved in 3 cups soymilk

1 teaspoon salt, or to taste

Per 2 cups: Calories 226, Total Protein 18 g, Soy Protein 15 g, Carbohydrates 31 g, Fat 3 g, Sodium 655 mg

Triple Onion Soup

Yield 10 cups

uring the preparation of this soup, my tear ducts worked overtime. It was well worth it, however, for this creamy soup is full of flavor.

4 cups chopped leeks

4 cups chopped onions

3 tablespoons chopped garlic

1 tablespoon soy margarine

6 cups water

1 teaspoon thyme

½ teaspoon celery seed

1 (12.3-ounce) package firm silken tofu

2 scoops GeniSoy Natural Protein Powder (½ cup)

½ cup nutritional yeast

2 tablespoons soy sauce

1 teaspoon salt

Remember to slit the leeks up the center so you can wash inbetween the upper leaves. You can chop up to where the green part gets tough.

Sauté the garlic and onions in the margarine for 10 minutes, stirring constantly until the vegetables are soft. Remove ¾ cup of the sautéed vegetables to add back later.

Add the water and spices, and bring to a boil. Cook for 10 minutes at a low boil.

Blend the tofu and protein powder along with the contents of the soup pot. Do this in several batches so the soup won't overflow the blender jar. Return the puréed soup to the pot.

Add the nutritional yeast, soy sauce, salt, and the reserved sautéed vegetables to the creamy soup. Mix well and bring just up to a boil, then turn the heat off and cover for several minutes before serving.

Per 2 cups: Calories 87, Total Protein 15 g, Soy Protein 15 g, Carbohydrates 2 g, Fat 2 g, Sodium 542 mg

Stick-To-Your-Ribs Chili

Yield: about 1 quart (4 servings)

Nothing satisfies quite like a steaming "bowl of red." The bulgur in this recipe adds a "meaty" chewiness that complements the soft, rich texture of the beans. Don't be daunted by the lengthy list of ingredients—it primarily consists of seasonings. This recipe is nothing less than simple and delicious, and it will win you raves every time. Serve it with corn muffins, baked corn chips, or biscuits.

Place the olive oil in a 4½-quart saucepan or Dutch oven, and heat it over medium-high. When the oil is hot, add the onion, celery, and garlic. Reduce the heat to medium, and cook, stirring occasionally, for 10 to 15 minutes, or until the onion is tender.

When the onion is tender, stir in the remaining ingredients, except the salt and protein powder, and bring the mixture to a boil. Reduce the heat to low, cover the saucepan with a lid, and simmer the chili for 20 minutes, stirring occasionally.

Stir in the protein powder, and season the chili with salt to taste. Serve hot.

2 teaspoons olive oil

1 cup finely chopped onion

½ cup finely chopped celery

2 cloves garlic, minced or pressed

2 ripe medium tomatoes, peeled, seeded and coarsely chopped

1 (15-ounce) can red kidney beans, pinto beans or black beans (about 1½ cups), rinsed well and drained

1 (8-ounce) can tomato sauce (1 cup), or ⅓ cup tomato paste mixed with ⅔ cup water

1 cup water

⅓ cup bulgur (medium ground)

2 tablespoons tomato paste

1 tablespoon sweetener of your choice

1 tablespoon chili powder

½ teaspoon dried oregano leaves

¼ teaspoon ground black pepper

¼ teaspoon ground cumin

⅛ teaspoon ground allspice or cinnamon

Pinch of cayenne pepper, to taste

1 scoop GeniSoy Natural Protein Powder (¼ cup)

Salt, to taste

Tips: To peel a tomato, first use a sharp knife to cut a small cross on the bottom of the tomato. Turn the tomato over and cut out the core. Immerse the tomato in a pot of boiling water for about 20 seconds. Remove the tomato from the pot using a slotted spoon, and transfer it to a bowl of cold water. Let it rest for 1 minute. Remove the tomato from the cold water, and peel off the skin using your fingers—it should peel away easily.

To seed a tomato, cut the tomato in half crosswise, and gently squeeze out the seeds.

If you prefer a milder chili, go easy on the black pepper and cayenne, or eliminate them completely.

For added sweetness and texture, stir in 1 grated carrot and/or a few raisins before bringing the mixture to a boil.

Per serving: Calories 285, Total Protein 17 g, Soy Protein 6 g, Carbohydrates 47 g, Fat 2 g, Sodium 465 mg

Pasta Primavera Salad

Yield: 6 to 8 servings

H ere's a hearty full-meal salad that's good enough to serve to company.

Cook the pasta in a large pot of boiling, salted water. While it cooks, prepare the vegetables. When the pasta is almost half-cooked, add the raw carrots to the pot of simmering pasta. When the pasta is almost tender, add the green beans (and frozen carrot slices, if using). When the pasta is just tender, but still chewy, drain it with the carrots and green beans in a colander.

Place the drained pasta and vegetables in a large serving bowl with the onion, beans, peppers, tomatoes, and celery. Add the 2 tablespoons vinegar, 1 teaspoon salt, and pepper to taste. Toss well. Place the dressing ingredients in a blender or food processor, and blend until very smooth. Pour it over the warm pasta, and combine well. Cover and refrigerate until serving time. Serve at room temperature or cold.

Salad

¾ pound dry penne, rotelle, or fusilli (corkscrew) pasta

2 medium carrots, peeled and cut into thin oval slices, or 3 cups frozen sliced carrots

½ pound frozen, whole, small green beans

1 large onion, chopped

1 (15-ounce) can red or white (cannellini) kidney beans, or chick-peas, drained (1½ cups cooked)

1 green bell pepper, seeded and diced

1 red bell pepper, seeded and diced

3 roma tomatoes, sliced

1 cup thinly sliced celery

2 tablespoons white wine vinegar

1 teaspoon salt

Freshly ground black pepper, to taste

Dressing

1 (12.3-ounce) box firm silken
  tofu

1 scoop GeniSoy Natural Protein
  Powder (¼ cup)

¼ cup lemon juice

¼ cup chopped fresh basil, or
  1½ tablespoons dried

1 tablespoon white wine
  vinegar

1 teaspoon salt

½ teaspoon dry mustard
  powder

*Per serving: Calories 224, Total Protein 14 g, Soy Protein 7 g,
Carbohydrates 37 g, Fat 2 g, Sodium 699 mg*

Grilled Cheeze Sandwiches

Yield: 4 sandwiches

This perennial kid-pleaser still has all the goo and glory that made it so outrageously popular, but now it's low-fat and dairy-free! We like to serve these with a dab of grainy mustard spread on top.

To make the Melty American Cheeze, place all the ingredients except the bread in a 2-quart saucepan, and whisk them together until the mixture is smooth. Bring the mixture to a boil, stirring constantly with the wire whisk. Reduce the heat to low, and continue to cook, stirring constantly, until the Melty American Cheeze is very thick and smooth. Remove the saucepan from the heat.

Place four of the bread slices on a flat surface. Cover one side of each of the bread slices evenly with the Melty American Cheeze. Top with the remaining bread slices.

Mist a large skillet with nonstick cooking spray, or coat it with a thin layer of canola oil. Place the skillet over medium-high heat. When the skillet is hot, add the sandwiches and brown them well on each side, carefully

Melty American Cheeze

⅔ cup water

6 tablespoons nutritional yeast flakes

2 tablespoons oat flour (blend dry oatmeal in your blender)

1 scoop GeniSoy Natural Protein Powder (¼ cup)

2 tablespoons fresh lemon juice

1½ tablespoons tomato paste or ketchup

1 teaspoon onion granules

½ teaspoon garlic granules

½ teaspoon turmeric

½ teaspoon dry mustard

½ teaspoon salt

8 slices whole grain bread

turning them over once with a metal spatula. (If all the sandwiches do not fit in the skillet at the same time, grill them in batches.)

Transfer the sandwiches to serving plates using the metal spatula. Slice the sandwiches in half diagonally, and serve them at once.

Per sandwich: Calories 180, Total Protein 15 g, Soy Protein 6 g, Carbohydrates 24 g, Fat 2 g, Sodium 292 mg

Nottuna

Yield: 2 to 4 servings

This chick-pea salad has a taste and texture reminiscent of tuna salad.

Place the chick-peas in a food processor fitted with a metal blade, and pulse until they are coarsely chopped.

Transfer the chopped beans to a medium mixing bowl, and stir in the remaining ingredients. Mix well. Serve the salad at once, or transfer it to a storage container, and chill it in the refrigerator.

1½ cups cooked or canned chick-peas (garbanzo beans), rinsed well and drained

¼ cup finely chopped celery

¼ cup finely chopped mild, sweet onions

2 to 3 tablespoons GeniSoy Natural Protein Powder stirred into 3 to 4 tablespoons of your favorite egg- and dairy-free mayonnaise

1 tablespoon nutritional yeast flakes

1 tablespoon fresh lemon juice

⅛ teaspoon paprika

Salt and ground black pepper, to taste

Per serving: Calories 211, Total Protein 12 g, Soy Protein 5 g, Carbohydrates 27 g, Fat 4 g, Sodium 196 mg

THE
MAGIC
OF SOY

Enchiladas

Yield: 4 to 6 servings

Use the tortillas on page 50 for this recipe or purchase ready-made ones.

To make the chile gravy, sauté the green pepper, onion, and garlic in the olive oil, add the chili powder.

In a blender, combine the water, protein powder, flour, and salt. Stir the blended mixture into the peppers and onion, and heat to simmering, while stirring constantly to avoid lumping.

To make the filling, sauté the onions, peppers, garlic, and cumin in the olive oil until tender. Process the beans, liquid, protein powder, and salt in a food processor until creamy.

Lay out the tortillas and divide the bean mixture evenly among them. Roll up the tortillas.

Preheat the oven to 350°F.

Pour half of the chili gravy into a 2-quart pan. Place the rolled tortillas in the pan in a row. Pour the rest of the gravy over the top, and bake for about 30 minutes.

Chili Gravy

1 cup chopped green pepper
1 cup chopped onion
2 cloves garlic, minced
1 tablespoon olive oil
2 tablespoons chili powder

3 cups water
1 scoop GeniSoy Natural Protein Powder (¼ cup)
1 tablespoon flour
1 teaspoon salt

Filling

1 cup chopped onions
1 cup chopped sweet peppers
2 cloves garlic minced
1 teaspoon cumin seeds
1 tablespoon olive oil
2 cups pinto beans or 1 (16-ounce) can, drained, liquid reserved
½ cup cooking water from beans
1 scoop GeniSoy Natural Protein Powder (¼ cup)
½ teaspoon salt
6 flour tortillas

Per serving: Calories 313, Total Protein 18 g, Soy Protein 10 g, Carbohydrates 42 g, Fat 8 g, Sodium 892 mg

Soyfelafel

Yield:15 balls

The tofu keeps these soft and moist inside even though they are baked. The quick baking at high heat makes them crispy on the outside.

1 medium onion

1 cup chopped fresh parsley, or ½ cup chopped fresh parsley plus ½ cup chopped fresh cilantro or mint

5 cloves garlic

1 cup cooked or canned drained chick-peas

½ pound medium-firm tofu

1½ cups loosely packed fresh bread crumbs

1 scoop GeniSoy Natural Protein Powder (¼ cup)

1 tablespoon lemon juice

2 teaspoons ground cumin

1½ teaspoons ground coriander

1 teaspoon salt

¼ teaspoon cayenne

Freshly ground black pepper, to taste

Preheat the oven to 500°F.

In a food processor, finely mince the onion, parsley, and garlic. Add the remaining ingredients and process briefly. Drop heaping tablespoonfuls onto 2 cookie sheets lightly covered with olive oil. Flatten each mound a little with an oiled spoon, keeping the edges of the patties as smooth and even as possible. Bake in the oven for 5 to 7 minutes until golden brown and crispy on the bottom. Turn the patties over and bake another 5 to 7 minutes until both sides are crispy and golden brown.

Serve in fresh whole wheat pita breads with either dark greens or sliced cucumber, tomato, and onion, and soy yogurt or mayonnaise and some hot sauce.

If you'd like to have a little more of a fried flavor, you can let the patties cool and then sauté them briefly in a nonstick skillet with about ½ to 1 tablespoon olive oil for each 7 or 8 balls.

Per 2 balls: Calories 102, Total Protein 8 g, Soy Protein 5 g, Carbohydrates 14 g, Fat 1 g, Sodium 385 mg

Greek-Style Spinach "Pizza"

Yield: 6 servings

This rather original "pizza" is a deliciously quick way to get the taste of spanikopita without all the messing around with phyllo pastry. Miso, tofu, and nutritional yeast give this filling an authentic feta-like flavor. You can use this filling to make actual vegan spanikopitas when you have time.*

Preheat the oven to 450°F.

Mix the tofu, protein powder, miso, and nutritional yeast together in a bowl with a potato masher. (Do not blend or process.) Add the remaining ingredients and mix together well. Spread the filling evenly over the crust. Decorate with red pepper slices, if you like. Bake on a nonstick or lightly oiled cookie sheet for 15 minutes.

* This amount of filling will fill 10 small triangles, 7 rolls, an 8-inch square spanikopita, or a 9 to 10-inch filled pie or open-faced quiche. Double the recipe for a 9 x 13-inch pan of spanikopita, 2 pies or quiches, 20 triangles, or 14 rolls. You can add a third package of spinach to the double recipe of filling if you like it more "green."

1 (12-inch) prebaked pizza or Italian flat bread crust (If you prefer, you can prepare a Pizza Crust, page 48)

Filling

¾ pound (12 ounces or 1½ cups) medium-firm tofu, or 1⅓ (12.3-ounce) boxes extra-firm silken tofu

1 scoop GeniSoy Natural Protein Powder (¼ cup)

2 tablespoons light miso

1 tablespoon nutritional yeast flakes

1 (10-ounce) package frozen chopped spinach, thawed and squeezed dry

⅔ cup finely chopped green onion stems (green part only)

1 tablespoon dry dillweed, or ¼ cup chopped fresh

½ teaspoon salt

Slices of red bell pepper to decorate the top (optional)

Per serving: Calories 163, Total Protein 14 g, Soy Protein 10 g, Carbohydrates 19 g, Fat 4 g, Sodium 404 mg

Tofu Burgers, Spaghetti Balls, or Tofu Loaf

Yield: 6 to 8 burgers, 18 balls, or 1 loaf

1 pound tofu, mashed or crumbled

½ cup rolled oats

1 small onion, chopped

2 cloves garlic, minced

1 scoop GeniSoy Natural Protein Powder (¼ cup)

¼ cup chopped fresh parsley

3 tablespoons soy sauce

1 teaspoon poultry seasoning, or ½ teaspoon sage plus ½ teaspoon thyme

Mix all the ingredients in a bowl.

For burgers, shape into 8 burgers and brown in 2 tablespoons oil.

For spaghetti balls, shape into 20 balls and brown in ½ cup oil.

For tofu loaf, preheat the oven to 350°F. Press the mix into an oiled loaf pan, top with ¼ cup ketchup, and bake for about 30 minutes. Let it cool for about 10 minutes before slicing. This makes good sandwiches cold or refried.

Per burger: Calories 97, Total Protein10 g, Soy Protein 8 g, Carbohydrates 7 g, Fat 3 g, Sodium 478 mg

Classic Quiche

Yield: 6 servings

 ou can vary this basic recipe by steaming 2 cups of broccoli, spinach, or mushrooms and adding to the filling before baking. The filling contains no eggs or dairy products, yet it's very creamy and rich tasting.

Preheat the oven to 350°F.

Blend all the ingredients for the filling in a food processor, or combine in a large bowl and process in 2 batches in a blender until completely smooth.

Heat the oil in a skillet over medium-high, and sauté the onion until tender and golden, about 8 minutes. Stir the onion and vegetarian bacon bits into the blended mixture, and pour into the prebaked pie crust. Bake for 40 to 45 minutes, or until the top is firm, browned, and slightly puffed. Allow the quiche to rest for 15 minutes before slicing.

Filling

2 (12.3-ounce) packages firm silken tofu, crumbled

¾ cup soymilk or water

2 scoops GeniSoy Natural Protein Powder (½ cup)

¼ cup nutritional yeast flakes

½ teaspoon salt

¼ teaspoon nutmeg

Scant ¼ teaspoon turmeric

⅛ teaspoon ground white pepper (optionals)

2 teaspoons canola oil

1½ cups finely chopped onion

⅔ cup vegetarian bacon bits

1 (9-inch) prebaked pie shell

Per serving: Calories 358, Total Protein 26 g, Soy Protein 17 g, Carbohydrates 25 g, Fat 16 g, Sodium 725 mg

Fettuccine Alfredo with Broccoli

Yield: 4 servings

oman restaurateur Alfredo di Lello is credited with creating this dish in the 1920s. Traditionally, fettuccine noodles are enrobed in a sauce of butter, Parmesan cheese, heavy cream, and sometimes egg yolks. This lighter version captures the rich taste of classic fettuccine Alfredo, but lets you indulge guilt-free.

Sauce

1½ cups crumbled firm silken tofu

1 scoop GeniSoy Natural Protein Powder (¼ cup)

2 to 3 tablespoons olive oil

2 tablespoons nutritional yeast flakes

1 tablespoon garlic granules

1 tablespoon lemon juice

½ teaspoon salt, or to taste

½ teaspoon Dijon mustard

12 ounces dry fettuccine noodles

2 cups bite-size broccoli florets

12 to 16 fresh basil leaves, torn (optional)

Ground black pepper, to taste

Make a garlic cream sauce by processing the crumbled tofu, protein powder, olive oil, nutritional yeast, garlic, lemon juice, salt, and Dijon mustard in a food processor or blender until completely smooth and creamy. Set aside.

Fill a 4-quart saucepan two-thirds full with water, bring to a rolling boil, and cook the fettuccine in it until it is almost al denté. Add the broccoli florets and cook until they are bright green. Drain the pasta and broccoli well, and return them to the saucepan.

Add the garlic cream sauce to the cooked pasta and broccoli, and toss well until they are evenly coated.

Divide the fettuccine among 4 warm plates or pasta bowls. Garnish each serving with the fresh basil leaves, if using, and ground black pepper. Serve at once.

Per serving: Calories 439, Total Protein 28 g, Soy Protein 14 g, Carbohydrates 50 g, Fat 13 g, Sodium 463 mg

Baked Macaroni & Cheeze

Yield: 4 to 6 servings

The American dish known as macaroni and cheese was created by Thomas Jefferson and became popularized during the 19th century. This cheese-free version has captured the rich taste and tang of traditional macaroni and cheese, yet it's totally dairy-free.

Preheat the oven to 375°F.

Mist an 8 x 8 x 2-inch square baking pan with nonstick cooking spray, and set it aside.

Cook the macaroni in boiling water until it is al denté. Drain it well and return it to the saucepan. Cover and set aside.

Meanwhile, prepare the sauce. Place the 2 tablespoons olive oil in a 2-quart saucepan, and heat over medium-high. Stir in the flour, protein powder, mustard, and cayenne pepper. Cook for 1 minute, stirring constantly.

Gradually stir in the heated milk, a little at a time, whisking constantly. (It will take about 5 to 7 minutes to add the milk. The sauce should continue to bubble as you add the milk; if it doesn't, you are adding the milk too quickly.) If necessary, cook the sauce until it is the consistency of thick cream, about 2 to 4 minutes longer. Remove from

2½ cups dry elbow macaroni

Sauce

2 tablespoons olive oil

⅓ cup whole wheat pastry flour

1 scoop GeniSoy Natural Protein Powder (¼ cup)

½ teaspoon dry mustard

Pinch of cayenne pepper

2½ cups soymilk, heated

½ cup nutritional yeast flakes

1 teaspoon salt

Ground black pepper, to taste

1 tablespoon minced fresh parsley, or 1 teaspoon dried parsley flakes (optional)

½ cup fresh, whole grain bread crumbs, packed

1 tablespoon olive oil (optional)

the heat and stir in the nutritional yeast flakes. Season with the salt and black pepper. Pour the sauce over the cooked macaroni, add the parsley, if using, and mix well.

Transfer the macaroni to the prepared baking pan. Sprinkle the bread crumbs evenly over the top, and drizzle with the remaining 1 tablespoon of olive oil, if desired. Bake for 25 to 30 minutes. Let stand for 5 minutes before serving.

Per serving: Calories 372, Total Protein 20 g, Soy Protein 8 g, Carbohydrates 52 g, Fat 8 g, Sodium 540 mg

Noodles Romanoff

Yield: 8 servings

This can be made ahead and reheated later. It is also ready to eat without the baking, if you are in a hurry.

Boil the noodles in salted water until al dente, and drain.

Preheat the oven to 350°F.

Sauté the onion and garlic in the olive oil until translucent.

Blend the soymilk and protein powder in a food processor or blender until smooth and creamy. Combine all the ingredients, and pour into a 2-quart baking dish. Bake for 15 to 20 minutes. Serve hot with more soy Parmesan on the side, if you like.

1 pound flat noodles

1 onion, chopped

2 cloves garlic, minced

¼ cup oil

2 cups soymilk

1½ scoops GeniSoy Natural Protein Powder (¼ cup plus 2 tablespoons)

½ pound tofu

1 cup chopped fresh parsley

6 tablespoons soy Parmesan

Salt, to taste

Per serving: Calories 224, Total Protein 14 g, Soy Protein 11 g, Carbohydrates 21 g, Fat 10 g, Sodium 178 mg

Lasagne

Yield: 4 servings

8 lasagne noodles (½ pound)

1 ounce fresh basil, chopped

1 small onion, chopped

2 cloves garlic, minced

1 pound firm tofu

3 tablespoons lemon juice

1 teaspoon salt

¼ cup nutritional yeast (optional)

2 tablespoons GeniSoy Natural Protein Powder

1 (26-ounce) jar pasta sauce

½ cup soy Parmesan

Boil the noodles in salt water until all dente, drain, rinse, and drain again.

Preheat the oven to 350°F.

Chop the basil, onion, and garlic in a food processor. Add the tofu, lemon juice, salt, nutritional yeast, and protein powder, and process until it is the consistency of ricotta cheese.

Pour half of the pasta sauce over the bottom of a 2-quart baking dish. Lay half of the noodles over the sauce. Spread the tofu mixture over the noodles, cover with the rest of the noodles, then spread the remaining pasta sauce over the top. Sprinkle the soy Parmesan over the top.

Bake for 35 to 45 minutes until bubbling.

Per serving: Calories 314, Total Protein 23 g, Soy Protein 17 g, Carbohydrates 38 g, Fat 7 g, Sodium 2057 mg

Scalloped Potatoes

Yield: 4 to 6 servings

Peel and slice the potatoes in a food processor or thinly by hand. Blend the soymilk, protein powder, salt, and pepper in a blender until smooth.

Preheat the oven to 350°F.

Build layers of sliced potatoes, then chopped onions, then dribble on the olive oil. Pour the soymilk mixture over all, and cover. Bake for 1½ to 2 hours or until the potatoes are soft.

6 white potatoes, thinly sliced (2 pounds)

3 cups soymilk

1½ scoops GeniSoy Natural Protein Powder (¼ cup plus 2 tablespoons)

2 teaspoons salt

½ teaspoon freshly ground black pepper

1 onion, chopped

2 tablespoons olive oil

Per serving: Calories 292, Total Protein 14 g, Soy Protein 11 g, Carbohydrates 41 g, Fat 8 g, Sodium 967 mg

Boofers

Yield: 12 patties (6 servings)

ou can make the mashed potatoes for these cakes from dehydrated potato flakes using soymilk in place of milk to boost the soy protein content.

1 onion, chopped

3 tablespoons oil

3 cups mashed potatoes (can be from dehydrated potato flakes)

½ pound tofu, crumbled

1½ scoops GeniSoy Natural Protein Powder (¼ cup plus 2 tablespoons)

½ cup minced fresh parsley

½ teaspoon salt

¼ teaspoon black pepper

Sauté the onion in 1 tablespoon of the oil until soft. Mix the onion into the potatoes along with the remaining ingredients. Shape into 12 patties ½ inch thick.

Brown on each side in the remaining 2 tablespoons oil.

Per serving: Calories 193, Total Protein 10 g, Soy Protein 9 g, Carbohydrates 19 g, Fat 8 g, Sodium 260 mg

Desserts

THE
MAGIC
OF SOY

Tofu Whipped Topping

Yield: about ¾ cup

This incredibly easy whipped topping has a mesmerizing flavor. Let it be the crowning touch to all your vegan confections.

Place all the ingredients in a blender or food processor fitted with a metal blade, and process until the mixture is completely smooth and very creamy.

Store the topping in a covered container in the refrigerator until you are ready to use it.

Tip: The secret to the ultra-creamy consistency of this topping is processing it for several minutes. This is necessary to pulverize the tofu thoroughly and eliminate any graininess. After the long processing time, the texture will be miraculously transformed. You may find that a food processor is easier to use if the mixture is too thick to process effectively in your blender.

¾ cup crumbled firm silken tofu

2 tablespoons GeniSoy Natural Protein Powder

2 tablespoons pure maple syrup

2 teaspoons hazelnut oil, walnut oil, or canola oil

1 teaspoon vanilla extract

Pinch of ground nutmeg

Per 2 tablespoons: Calories 61, Total Protein 5 g, Soy Protein 5 g, Carbohydrates 5 g, Fat 2 g, Sodium 37 mg

Sweetened Condensed Soymilk

Yield: 1⅔ cups (equal to 1 commercial 14-ounce can)

This can be used in baking and candy-making instead of canned condensed dairy milk. It's fast to make and keeps in the refrigerator for several weeks.

1 cup light unbleached sugar

⅔ cup boiling water

6 tablespoons soymilk powder

5 tablespoons GeniSoy Natural Protein Powder or GeniSoy Natural Vanilla Shake Powder

1 tablespoon melted soy margarine

Combine all the ingredients in a blender, and process until the sugar is dissolved and the mixture is thick. Pour into a clean jar, cover, and refrigerate. The milk thickens when chilled.

Per 2 tablespoons: Calories 86, Total Protein 4 g, Soy Protein 4 g, Carbohydrates 15 g, Fat 0 g, Sodium 38 mg

Mile-High Chocolate Layer Cake

Yield: 1 *three-layer cake* (12 to 14 *servings*)

This multilayered cake is a chocolate lover's fantasy come true.

Preheat the oven to 350°F.

Mist three 9-inch round cake pans with nonstick cooking spray, and set them aside.

Place the wet ingredients in a blender, and process until smooth. Place the dry ingredients in a large mixing bowl, and stir them together. Pour the wet ingredients into the dry ingredients, and beat well using a wire whisk or electric beater to make a smooth batter.

Pour the batter equally into the prepared baking pans, and bake until a cake tester inserted in the center of each cake comes out clean, about 25 to 30 minutes. Remove the pans from the oven, and place them on cooling racks. Allow the cakes to cool for 10 to 15 minutes. Then turn them out of the pans, and allow them to cool completely.

Wet Ingredients

1¾ cups sugar

1½ cups crumbled firm silken tofu

1 cup water

⅓ cup canola oil

2 teaspoons apple cider vinegar or lemon juice

1 teaspoon vanilla extract

Dry Ingredients

2 cups unbleached flour

½ cup unsweetened cocoa powder

2 scoops GeniSoy Natural Chocolate Shake Powder (½ cup)

1 tablespoon non-aluminum baking powder

¼ teaspoon salt

3 cups your favorite chocolate frosting

To frost the cake, place one of the layers on an attractive serving plate, flat side up. Spread the top of the layer carefully with ¼ of the frosting. Place the second cake layer, flat side up, on top of the first, and flatten gently with your hand. Spread the top of the second layer with ⅓ of the remaining frosting. Place the third layer, flat side up, on top and again flatten gently. Frost the top and sides of the cake using all of the remaining frosting. Using a flat-edged knife or icing spatula, make quick movements to create swirls on the top and sides of the cake. Let stand for about 1 hour to set the frosting. Serve at room temperature.

Per serving: Calories 258, Total Protein 7 g, Soy Protein 4 g, Carbohydrates 42 g, Fat 7 g, Sodium 80 mg

Sweet Dessert Creme

Yield: about ⅞ cup

delicious pourable cream for topping fruit and cake slices. The coconut extract doesn't make it taste like coconut, but gives the cream a rich flavor.

Combine all the ingredients in a blender, and process until very smooth.

This can be refrigerated for several days. Stir gently before using.

- ½ cup soymilk, rice milk, or almond milk
- ½ cup crumbled extra-firm silken tofu
- 2 tablespoons GeniSoy Natural Vanilla Shake Powder
- 4 teaspoons Grade A maple syrup
- Pinch salt
- 1 tablespoon canola oil
- ¼ teaspoon coconut extract

Per 2 tablespoons: Calories 54, Total Protein 3 g, Soy Protein 3 g, Carbohydrates 4 g, Fat2 g, Sodium 38 mg

Chocolate Frosting

Yield: 1 cup

This will frost a dozen cupcakes. Double it to frost a 9 x 13-inch sheet cake or 2-layer cake, and triple it to frost a 3-layer cake.

3 tablespoons soy margarine

2 tablespoons GeniSoy Natural Chocolate Shake Powder

⅓ cup unsweetened cocoa

1½ cups powdered sugar

¼ cup water or soymilk

1 teaspoon vanilla

Beat all the ingredients together until smooth and creamy. Add a little more liquid if needed to make a spreadable consistency.

Per 2 tablespoons: Calories 147, Total Protein 2 g, Soy Protein 1 g, Carbohydrates 25 g, Fat 5 g, Sodium 62 mg

Vanilla Frosting

Yield: 1¼ cups

Beat all the ingredients together until smooth and creamy. Add a little more liquid if needed.

3 tablespoons non-hydrogenated nondairy margarine

2 tablespoons GeniSoy Natural Vanilla Shake Powder

2 cups powdered sugar

3 tablespoons soymilk or water

1 teaspoon vanilla

Per 2 tablespoons: Calories 131, Total Protein 1 g, Soy Protein 1 g, Carbohydrates 24 g, Fat 3 g, Sodium 40 mg

Orange Frosting

Yield: 1¼ cups

Beat all the ingredients together until smooth and creamy. Add a little more liquid if needed.

3 tablespoons non-hydrogenated nondairy margarine

2 tablespoons GeniSoy Natural Vanilla Shake Powder

2 cups powdered sugar

1 teaspoon vanilla

4 tablespoons orange juice concentrate

Per 2 tablespoons: Calories 144, Total Protein 1 g, Soy Protein 1 g, Carbohydrates 27 g, Fat 3 g, Sodium 49 mg

Chocolate Sauce

Yield: 1⅓ cups

This easy sauce can be used to flavor drinks or to drizzle over frozen desserts, cakes, and puddings.

1 cup hot water or non-dairy milk

1 cup sugar

⅔ cup unsweetened cocoa

1 scoop GeniSoy Natural Chocolate Shake Powder (¼ cup)

2 teaspoons vanilla extract

Pour all the ingredients, except the vanilla, into a small, heavy saucepan, and stir over medium-high heat until it comes to a boil. Simmer, stirring, for 1 minute. Stir in the vanilla extract. Cool and store in a covered jar in the refrigerator. This will keep for several weeks.

Per 2 tablespoons: Calories 108, Total Protein 3 g, Soy Protein 1 g, Carbohydrates 22 g, Fat 0 g, Sodium 19 mg

Pumpkin Pie

Yield: 8 servings

I've been serving this pie for several years, and no one realizes that it's non-dairy and egg-free. It's very important to make this the day before you serve it so that the filling can set properly.

Preheat the oven to 350°F.

Combine all the filling ingredients in a large bowl, and process in 2 batches in a blender until smooth.

Combine the batches in a medium bowl, and pour into the unbaked pie crust.

Bake for 60 minutes. Cover the edges of the pie crust with foil if they begin to brown too quickly.

Cool on a rack, then refrigerate overnight before serving. Top with soy whipped topping, if desired.

Filling

2 cups canned or cooked pumpkin

1 cup non-dairy milk

¾ cup brown sugar

1 scoop GeniSoy Natural Vanilla Shake Powder (¼ cup)

1 tablespoon molasses

1 teaspoon cinnamon

½ teaspoon powdered ginger

½ teaspoon nutmeg

¼ teaspoon cloves

¼ teaspoon salt

1 teaspoon vanilla extract

1 (9-inch) unbaked pie crust

Per serving: Calories 247, Total Protein 4 g, Soy Protein 3 g, Carbohydrates 37 g, Fat 9 g, Sodium 281 mg

Chocolate Tofu Pie

Yield: 8 servings

2 (12.3-ounce) packages extra-firm silken tofu

⅔ cup sugar

2 scoops GeniSoy Natural Chocolate Shake Powder (½ cup)

1 teaspoon vanilla extract

6 ounces chocolate chips

1 (9-inch) graham cracker crust, baked

In a food processor, blend the tofu, sugar, protein powder, and vanilla extract until smooth and creamy.

Melt the chocolate chips on high power in a microwave oven for 1½ minutes. Add the melted chocolate chips to the blended ingredients in the food processor, and process again until blended.

Pour the mixture into the baked crust, and smooth with a spatula to fit into the shell. Chill for at least 4 hours or overnight.

Per serving: Calories 311, Total Protein 11 g, Soy Protein 9 g, Carbohydrates 48 g, Fat 17 g, Sodium 252 mg

Tofu Cheezecake Pie

Yield: 8 servings

Even people who haven't been able to warm up to tofu in any other form will find this delicious. Make this the day before serving.

Preheat the oven to 350°F.

Blend all the filling ingredients in a food processor, or combine them in a large mixing bowl and process in 2 batches in a blender until very smooth. Pour the mixture into the crumb crust, and bake for about 50 minutes, or until the mixture is set. Cool on a rack, then refrigerate until well chilled.

To make the fruit topping, mix the the frozen berries, sweetener, and cornstarch mixture in a small saucepan. Stir over high heat until it has boiled and thickened. Spoon the fruit topping over the cheezecake pie, and refrigerate until the topping is cool. Serve with soy whipped topping, if desired.

Filling

1 pound firm tofu

⅓ cup sugar

2 tablespoons soymilk

1 scoop GeniSoy Natural Vanilla Shake Powder (¼ cup)

1 tablespoon lemon juice

¼ teaspoon salt

1 teaspoon vanilla extract

½ teaspoon almond extract (optional)

½ teaspoon grated lemon zest (optional)

1 (9-inch) crumb crust

Fruit topping

2 cups frozen berries or other fruit

¼ to ½ cup sweetener of your choice

1 tablespoon cornstarch mixed with 2 tablespoons cold water

Per serving: Calories 281, Total Protein 7 g, Soy Protein 6 g, Carbohydrates 37 g, Fat 11 g, Sodium 271 mg

Cherry Cobbler

Yield: 4 to 6 servings

1 (17-ounce) can pitted red tart cherries, drained, with juice reserved

⅔ cup sugar

1 cup unbleached flour

1 teaspoon non-aluminum baking powder

2 scoops GeniSoy Natural Vanilla Shake Powder (½ cup)

1 cup soymilk

Preheat the oven to 350°F.

Drain the cherry liquid into a small saucepan, and stir in ⅓ cup of the sugar. Bring to a boil over low heat. Mix together the flour, baking powder, protein, powder, and remaining sugar in a food processor. While the food processor is running, pour in the soymilk and process just until it is mixed in.

Pour the batter into an oiled 8 x 8-inch square or round pan. Sprinkle the drained cherries over the top evenly. Pour the boiling sweetened cherry liquid over the top of all, and bake for about 45 minutes, or until the middle springs back to the touch of a finger and it is browned.

Per serving: Calories 295, Total Protein 10 g, Soy Protein 7 g, Carbohydrates 61 g, Fat 1 g, Sodium 81 mg

Vanilla Rolled Cookies

Yield: thirty 3-inch cookies

Preheat the oven to 350°F.

Cream together the brown sugar, oil, tofu, protein powder, and vanilla in a food processor or by hand in a small mixing bowl.

Mix the flour, baking powder, and salt together in a medium bowl. Add to the creamed ingredients, and either pulse only until blended (about 10 pulses) or mix in with a whisk.

Roll out ¼ inch thick, and cut into shapes. Place on cookie sheets, and bake for 8 to 10 minutes. Decorate when cooled.

¾ cup brown sugar

¼ cup oil

¼ pound soft tofu

2 scoops GeniSoy Natural Vanilla Shake Powder (½ cup)

2 teaspoons vanilla

2 cups unbleached white flour

2 teaspoons non-aluminum baking powder

½ teaspoon salt

Per cookie: Calories 67, Total Protein 2 g, Soy Protein 1 g, Carbohydrates 10 g, Fat 2 g, Sodium 50 mg

Fudgy Cocoa Cookies

Yield: 48 cookies

Zucchini helps make these fudgy, chewy cookies moist. They are moister and chewier the second day, if they last that long. Peppermint, coffee, or coconut extract can be substituted for the peppermint.

1¾ cups unbleached or whole wheat flour, or half and half of each

3 scoops GeniSoy Natural Chocolate Shake Powder (¾ cup)

½ cup unsweetened cocoa

2 teaspoons baking soda

¼ teaspoon salt

¼ cup oil

1½ cups sugar

1 teaspoon peppermint extract

3 cups finely grated zucchini

1 cup broken walnuts (optional)

Preheat the oven to 350°F.

Mix the flour, protein powder, cocoa, baking soda, and salt together in a bowl.

Beat the oil, sugar, zucchini, and peppermint extract together with a mixer. Add the dry ingredients and beat until smooth. Fold in the walnuts.

Drop by tablespoonfuls onto cookie sheets, and bake for about 12 minutes.

Per cookie: Calories 59, Total Protein 2 g, Soy Protein 1 g, Carbohydrates 11 g, Fat 1 g, Sodium 22 mg

Chocolate Chip Bars

Yield: 2 dozen bars

Preheat the oven to 350°F.

Mix together the flours, baking powder, baking soda, and salt in a bowl.

In a mixer, beat together the tofu, brown sugar, oil, vanilla, and protein powder until creamy. Add the flour mixture and beat until blended. Add the chocolate chips and nuts, and beat again just until blended.

Spread the batter into a 9 x 13-inch pan, and bake for 20 to 25 minutes, or until golden brown.

2 cups unbleached flour

½ cup whole wheat flour

1 teaspoon non-aluminum baking powder

½ teaspoon baking soda

½ teaspoon salt

1 (12.3-ounce) package firm silken tofu, crumbled

1 cup brown sugar

½ cup oil

2 teaspoons vanilla

2 scoops GeniSoy Natural Vanilla Shake Powder (½ cup)

1 cup chocolate chips

½ cup chopped walnuts or pecans

Per serving: Calories 176, Total Protein 4 g, Soy Protein 2 g, Carbohydrates 21 g, Fat 9 g, Sodium 68 mg

Nut Butter Cookies

Yield: 48 cookies

1 cup peanut, almond, soynut, or cashew butter

1 cup granulated sweetener

¼ cup GeniSoy Natural Vanilla Shake Powder or GeniSoy Natural Protein Powder

½ cup oil

½ cup soymilk

½ teaspoon vanilla

2 cups flour

2 teaspoons non-aluminum baking powder

½ teaspoon salt

Preheat the oven to 350°F.

Beat together the nut butter, sweetener, and protein powder with an electric mixer.

Beat in the rest of the ingredients until well blended. Roll into 48 balls and flatten with a fork dipped in water, making cross marks.

Bake on cookie sheets for 10 to 12 minutes until browned.

Per cookie: Calories 86, Total Protein 3 g, Soy Protein 2 g, Carbohydrates 9 g, Fat 5 g, Sodium 30 mg

Dessert Crêpes

Yield: 6 (10-inch) crêpes

Stir the dry ingredients together in a bowl. Pour in the soymilk and whip. Add 1½ teaspoons of the oil to a hot non-stick crêpe pan, then roll and turn the pan to cover the bottom with the oil.

Pour in ½ cup of the crêpe batter, and immediately roll and turn the pan so it is evenly covered with the batter. Cook over medium-high heat until the crêpe starts to bubble and pull away from the sides of the pan. Carefully loosen the crêpe at the edges and flip over to cook the other side until it show flecks of golden color.

Prepare the remaining crêpe batter the same way. Serve hot.

Dry ingredients

1½ scoops GeniSoy Natural Vanilla Shake Powder (½ cup plus 2 tablespoons)

6 tablespoons unbleached flour

¼ teaspoon salt

2 cups vanilla soymilk

1 tablespoon oil

Per crêpe: Calories 104, Total Protein 7 g, Soy Protein 6 g, Carbohydrates 11 g, Fat 3 g, Sodium 144 mg

Index

Can't find *GeniSoy* products in your area stores?

The Mail Order Catalog for Healthy Eating

is your source for
GeniSoy Soy Protein
Powders and Shakes,
Protein Bars,
and Dry-Roasted Nuts.

THE
MAIL ORDER
CATALOG
FOR
HEALTHY EATING

For a free catalog: 1-800-695-2241
Online Shopping: www.healthy-eating.com
P.O. Box 180, Summertown, TN 38483

GeniSoy

SOY PROTEIN PRODUCTS

The Magic of Soy®

GeniSoy
SoyNuts!

GeniSoy SoyNuts are toasted to perfection without oil, have 60% less fat than peanuts and are available in Barbecue, Hickory Smoked, Salted & Unsalted.

GeniSoy products are made from certified non-GMO soybeans and are certified Kosher.

GeniSoy
Protein Powder & Shakes

The Rich Chocolate and Creamy Vanilla Shakes and Protein Powder are all natural. They're made from water processed Isolated Soy Protein and contain no yeast, wheat gluten, egg, dairy or animal derivatives.

For More Info, Call 1.888.GENISOY (436.4769) or Visit www.genisoy.com

The Magic of Soy®

GeniSoy
Protein Bars

Eight delicious flavors,
each providing 14 grams
of high quality, Isolated
Soy Protein with no
gluten or cholesterol

Heart Healthy 25 grams of soy protein a day, as part of a diet low in saturated fat and cholesterol, may reduce the risk of heart disease.

GeniSoy
Nature Grains Bars

Oven-Baked and All Natural,
it's the newest member of
the GeniSoy Family.
Available in Oatmeal
Raisin, Wild Berry,
Banana Nut & Chocolate,
they're all low-fat,
heart healthy & non-GMO.

GeniSoy Products, Inc • Fairfield, CA 94533

Purchase these soyfoods cookbooks at your local bookstore or natural foods store, or from:

Book Publishing Company
P.O. Box 99
Summertown, TN 38483
1-888-260-8458
www.bookpubco.com
Please include $3.50 shipping per book.

Tofu & Soyfoods Cookery - $12.95

Tofu Cookery - $15.95

Soyfoods Cookery - $9.95

The TVP® Cookbook - $7.95

Soyfoods Cooking for a Positive Menopause - $12.95

I Can't Believe It's Not Meat - $9.95